Other titles in the
Studies in English Language series

A Course Book in English Grammar – Dennis Freeborn

From Old English to Standard English – Dennis Freeborn

Varieties of English, 2nd Edition – Dennis Freeborn, *with Peter French and David Langford*

English Language Project Work – Christine McDonald

Series Standing Order

If you would like to receive future titles in this series as they are published, you can make use of our standing order facility. To place a standing order please contact your bookseller or, in case of difficulty, write to us at the address below with your name and address and the name of the series. Please state with which title you wish to begin your standing order. (If you live outside the United Kingdom we may not have the rights for your area, in which case we will forward your order to the publisher concerned.)

Standing Order Service, Macmillan Distribution Ltd,
Houndmills, Basingstoke, Hampshire, RG21 2XS, England

ANALYSING TALK

INVESTIGATING VERBAL INTERACTION IN ENGLISH

David Langford

MACMILLAN

First published 1994 by
THE MACMILLAN PRESS LTD
Houndmills, Basingstoke, Hampshire RG21 2XS
and London
Companies and representatives
throughout the world

ISBN 0-333-61494-1 hardcover
ISBN 0-333-42859-5 paperback

A catalogue record for this book is available from the British Library.

Printed in China

Contents

HAVANT
COLLEGE
LIBRARY

Acknowledgements

The author and publishers are grateful to Dr John Lee of the University of Manchester and Dr Anthony Wootton of the University of York for kind permission to base transcriptions on their recordings.

Every effort has been made to trace all copyright-holders, but if any have been inadvertently overlooked the publishers will be pleased to make the necessary arrangement at the first opportunity.

Preface

The study of language has traditionally focused on the grammatical, lexical and phonological features of particular languages or language varieties. It is in these areas that systematic patterning has been most evident and describable. It was assumed that the use of language in verbal interaction was not subject to predictable patterning. However, the investigation of how people interact verbally with one another has become over recent years an increasingly important part of language study. We do make sense of each other as a matter of routine in all sorts of interaction and in making sense of each other we go beyond the words used. The investigation of how people interact verbally amounts to the investigation of the ways in which we go beyond the words used.

This book sets out to provide beginning students of language use with a guide to setting about their own descriptions of how speakers in particular interactions have behaved in systematic ways and made sense of each others' behaviour. Records of interaction that have been collected by myself, colleagues and students and used in teaching form the basic data of the guide. Transcriptions have been made of material privately recorded or publicly broadcast. Care has been taken to acknowledge the original data sources but given the nature of the material this has not always been possible.

The general analytical approach adopted is derived from the work of conversation analysts such as Paul Drew, Anthony

Wooton, Gail Jefferson, Anita Pomerantz and Emanuel Schegloff. However, the book has concentrated on practical approaches to data analysis rather than on the substantive findings of researchers in the field. The aim has been to demonstrate that there is exciting research potential in any record of conversation and that the skills needed for original description can be developed by individuals working at quite different levels of sophistication in language study.

I do hope that the reading of this book will begin to bring into sharper focus the richness and complexity of everyday verbal interaction.

For those who wish to familiarise themselves with current research, other works have been more concerned to reflect the range of investigations into verbal interaction that have been informed by the approach presented here. In particular the reader's attention is drawn to Robert E. Nofsinger's *Everyday Conversation* (1991) for an accessible recent summary.

DAVID LANGFORD

1. Talk and its place in our lives

1.1 Introduction

For most of us the use of language is a crucial part of our daily lives. I'm a teacher so it's perhaps not at all surprising that language should play a particularly large part in what I do each day. Teaching might well be described with some accuracy as one of society's 'talking professions'. Working in the law, psychiatry, the media or a host of other areas could be similarly described. But with just a little reflection it soon becomes clear that nobody, whatever their age, social background, way of life or job, can for long avoid the use of language from the moment they wake until the moment they fall to sleep, and even then they may well dream of situations in which the use of language is again unavoidable. Using language is very much a part of what it is to be human and live the life of a human being.

This book will explore ways in which one particular, but perhaps the most familiar, aspect of language use can be investigated. I will be demonstrating ways in which you can set about the investigation and analysis of the everyday **talk** of ordinary people in a variety of more or less ordinary situations. You should discover that the skills people use in producing and understanding everyday talk are far from ordinary.

But first, to see just how pervasive all forms of language use can be in daily life, let's look in some detail at how it enters into a day in the life of just one individual – me. I shall attempt to construct a profile of how I use language in the course of one day and present it in the form of a narrative. (For the purposes of this exercise I am assuming that it's the middle of winter, a Monday morning, and that I was late in going to bed.)

1.2 A profile of a language user

A linguistic day in the life of David Langford

I wake with my alarm. I say to myself, but not out loud, a word or two that perhaps should not be printed here. I stagger to the bathroom, shave and generally prepare myself for the first phase of the day. Some of this is done in an entirely automatic fashion but some actions are actually the subject of silent but verbal planning. I might, for example, think to myself, by saying it to myself, that the blade in my razor is somewhat worn and should be changed. Furthermore, whilst performing the purely automatic actions I might well be thinking, in words, of my plans for the day – what I shall eat for breakfast, perhaps, or what I shall say in my first lecture of the day.

In addition to the silent language I am myself responsible for producing in my own head I will almost certainly and at the same time be encountering the silent, because written, language of the packaging of the typical household products to be found in the typical family bathroom. The toothpaste tube will bear a message about plaque and the merits of daily brushing. The shampoo bottle will bear a message about greasy hair. And underarm roll-on deodorant will bear a message about personal freshness. These messages I will certainly encounter as language, rather than, say, just any old marks on the surfaces of the packagings, even though I might not actually interpret the language for its meaning, still less interpret it as in some way a signal of the intended meanings of any particular individuals.

Having prepared myself for the day I go down to the kitchen and there, in the process of preparing my breakfast, encounter yet more written messages as they silently scream at me from food manufacturers' packets, bottles and cartons. I turn on the portable television set, strategically placed on a worktop, so as not to miss any vital bit of breakfast television whilst standing guard over slowly simmering porridge. I now encounter not my language, but the language of other people specifically produced by them as a means of communicating something to me along with several million others.

The language these people produce is mostly spoken language and whilst sometimes it is directed at me as if I were a partner in a conversation they are holding, at other times the language is directed at actual conversational partners, either present in the studio or linked by microphones, TV monitors and other electronic wizardry. But the odd thing is that whilst the talk is produced, for example, as part of a conversation involving just those who are indeed in the studio I nevertheless get the impression that the conversation is being produced specifically for me, and millions like me, as a potential overhearing audience. Furthermore, the participants in such talk somehow make it clear through the way that they talk that this is precisely the sort of impression they want me to be having.

However, whether the talk I encounter on the television is directly or just indirectly addressed to me I can only be a recipient of what I hear. I cannot talk back to a television and hope thereby to communicate with the people whose images I see on it. As yet such a possibility is not within the capability of the domestic television set. No doubt it will come – and, given the current pace of technological advance, sooner rather than later.

So far, then, I have encountered language and myself used language in a variety of forms. I have encountered language in written form, in broadcast spoken form, and I have used language to formulate my unspoken thoughts. What I have not done is to use language myself in order to communicate with another human being. All this is about to change as my two-year-old daughter pads into the room in her bear-like sleeping suit apparently demanding that I transform myself into a horse or other animal. Precisely which animal doesn't seem to matter too much so long as it can be sat upon, kicked, ridden and otherwise abused.

This whole episode, occurring as it does just as I'm attempting to take in the details of the television news summary whilst at the same time scanning the headlines of my large and difficult-to-handle *Guardian* newspaper, presents me with linguistic and interactional problems of a particular and difficult kind. For one thing, just what do the sounds and gestures the child is producing actually mean? Perhaps they have no precise meaning. How can I get the child to specify in more detail precisely what she wants when all the time I know the child can well be having similar difficulties in knowing precisely what my own probably unfamiliar words put together in not altogether familiar ways can mean? I know in some vague sort of way that she wants me to do something for her. But a further problem I have is that I don't want to do the thing right now because I have other, more pressing things on my mind. Simply to say *No!* might well upset the child. My aim must then be to manage things through my talk in such a way that this doesn't happen.

My much older daughter now appears. She agrees, but only after some delicate negotiation, to pick up some things for me at the chemist's shop on the way home from her sixth form college. I hurriedly write out a list for her.

My daughter and I then leave the house and get into the family car. My daughter is learning to drive and each day begins with her driving to college with me in the role of driving instructor. In this role I find myself using language to direct her actions, to encourage her, and inevitably sometimes to give rent to fearful anger. Needless to say my daughter is rarely a silent, non-reacting listener to my talk.

Having left my daughter at her college I drive on to my place of work. The car radio is tuned to my favourite 'talk' station. More news, more views, more interviews. Again, some of the talk is directed at me as if I were a non-responding conversational partner and some of the talk is directed primarily at studio-bound conversational partners – albeit with myself and millions of other listeners as an intended overhearing, though not seeing, audience. I interpret the talk I hear without responding – indeed the talk is continuous with, of course, no spaces being provided in which members of the audience might respond if and when the fancy took them. At the same time my eyes encounter written roadside messages in the form of signs, directions, advertising on hoardings, graffiti on walls and the like.

On this particular morning I have to visit a school on my way to work. The school happens to be in an area of the city that I don't know very well. So at the first opportunity I pull over to ask a passing pedestrian for directions. The noise of rumbling lorries doesn't make our brief exchange of talk the easiest of conversations.

Eventually I find the school and I spend a good half-hour with the headmaster discussing possibilities for teaching-practice placements for my students. At first he is reluctant because of the extra amount of work that it might involve for him and his staff but finally he comes round. We move on to less-business-related matters. These he seems to warm to and in fact he turns out to be the type of person who, given half a chance, just rambles on and on. Consequently, I now find myself in the difficult position of having to bring our meeting to a close without appearing abrupt, ungrateful, or in any other way giving offence.

Finally, I arrive at my own place of work to be greeted by a pile of internal memos, computer print-outs, letters and scribbled telephone messages. I spend the first half-hour at my desk writing memos, letters and returning telephone calls. It occurs to me that most of these memos, letters and telephone calls involve me either in getting other people to do things or in avoiding agreeing to do the things other people are trying to get me to do. We lead each other a merry communicational dance sometimes.

Around mid-morning I break for coffee which I take in the crowded common room with colleagues. As we drink our coffee my colleagues and I fill the air with the hubbub of reminders, arrangements, complaints and the whisper of shop gossip. The competition for speaking space in a ten-minute break with so much to be said can be as intense as the competition for eating-space among squealing pigs at the trough.

After coffee I give a lecture during which a group of 40 people must listen to my continuous talk which I consciously put together in such a way as to strike a balance between formality, clarity and interest. For the most part people listen in silence. If they do make any sort of response to what I say then the responses are self-directed in that they are the silently spoken responses of thought or hastily scribbled notes. At odd moments I reflect on these self-directed thoughts and wonder what relation there is between each of the 40 individual responses, the 40 scribbled interpretations of what I've said and what I actually meant by what I said. And again I wonder just what relation there will be between my students' essays, the scribbled notes the essays are based on and what I meant when I delivered my lecture. I am often surprised by the extent to which these responses, interpretations and meanings can differ given that everyone involved usually speaks the same language.

At the end of the lecture I invite, receive and respond to a range of questions before issuing instructions on preparatory work for the following week's topic.

During my lunch-break I join some friends to play a game of five-a-side soccer. Language, it seems, has a role to play here too and I finish the game with a voice that's hoarse and with a definite feeling that I'm rather less fit than I thought I was at the outset. A quick shower and banter and then over to the snack-bar to buy something to eat and drink before my first task of the afternoon. I am to interview a candidate for entry to College. No one taught me how to do this but somehow both the candidate and myself seem to know what's expected of each of us in the situation. The candidate happens to be a young woman and I remember having recently read a set of guidelines on how male interviewers should conduct themselves when talking to females. It seems that men and women actually adjust their ways of talking depending on whether their conversational partners are of the same or opposite sex. In particular it has been observed that men can adopt an especially patronising way of talking in interviews where the interviewee is female. I make a mental note to make sure that I talk in a way that I would expect another man to talk to me. But noting it is perhaps more difficult than doing it.

Immediately following the interview I have to lead a seminar. This involves me in trying to keep ten people talking on the same subject and, moreover, developing the talk on the subject in a direction that I want it to go whilst ensuring that everyone either takes the opportunity to talk or at least has the opportunity to talk.

My next job of the day is to attend a College committee meeting. I need to take a document with me. The document is held in my office computer which I use as a word-processor. I call up the document, make some minor changes and then print it out. The College committee meeting is an extremely formal affair with around 20 people in attendance. The organisation of the agenda means that I must wait for nearly an hour before the matter of interest to me is addressed. Finally I get to speak for something like 60 seconds. The agenda moves on and so do I.

I pop back to my office to pick up some papers I intend to read through at home later in the evening. At my door I find a rather distraught-looking second-year student. It turns out that he has just been told by his girlfriend that she wants their relationship to end. He is devastated and his immediate reaction is to talk in terms of leaving College. I listen sympathetically to his troubles as he relates them and do my best to offer counsel and advice.

The drive home is spent listening to a live broadcast of a cricket commentary. It's just as well that I learned the language of cricket at an early age. Otherwise the description of what is going on would make no sense at all. The description of the intermittent play is interspersed yet again with that kind of conversation which is produced by the likes of commentary teams precisely to be overheard.

At home my wife and I exchange descriptions of our day's troubles, triumphs and tedium as we jointly prepare food, with it never becoming fully clear just who is the skivvy and who the expert chef.

And whilst all this is going on the two-year-old's talk has to be encouraged, made sense of and responded to. After dinner, bedtime stories and bath-time I settle down to read, comment on and assess a pile of student essays. The process seems to take forever but I finish just in time to catch the beginning of my favourite TV soap – the kind of show that seeks to depict ordinary days in the lives of fictional people through their fictional talk. The ordinary days that are depicted seem familiar enough, but I'm struck by how extraordinarily good with words the characters always appear to be.

A friend rings just to confirm an arrangement for the weekend, or so he says. But somehow or other we get to talk about the state of English cricket, the problems of domestic life in general, and the problems of his own domestic life in particular. The call seems to go on and on and my daughter, who is waiting for a call herself, is not at all happy. An argument follows. Exhausted, I go to bed.

There follow a brief few minutes with my own bedtime book before drifting off to sleep, no doubt to dream of conversations I might have had, arguments I might have won, or things I might have said or written.

1.3 Language producers and language consumers

The description of a very ordinary day in my life, I think, clearly demonstrates the central and pervasive importance that language has for me: central in importance because it is so much a part of the work I do and pervasive because language plays a part in just about everything that I do. It is equally clear that not all uses of language during the course of an ordinary day will be similar. Sometimes language will be produced or encountered (let's say *consumed*) as written, sometimes it will be consumed as spoken and sometimes it will be consumed as imagined, e.g. as silent thought.

Activity 1.1

Examine the description of a linguistic day in my life and identify the situations in which I am a producer of language, the situations in which I am a consumer of language, and the situations in which I am both.

Activity 1.2

Now, in pairs, interview one another and provide a profile of a linguistic day in each other's life.

1.4 Writing, reading, speaking, listening

We can be either producers or consumers of written language – writers or readers. Similarly we can be either producers or consumers of spoken language – speakers or listeners. When we write we can do so with no expectation whatsoever of a direct response. This would be the case, for example, for the writer of a newspaper article. On the other hand we might write precisely with the expectation of a direct response. This would be the case for the writer of a memo to a colleague at work or for the writer of a shopping list produced as an instruction to someone else in the family.

And when we speak we can do so with no expectation whatsoever of a direct response that would involve someone else acting in some specific way. This would be the case, for example, for the radio or television newsreader. Or, again, we can speak precisely with the expectation of a direct and particular sort of response as when a doctor, for example, asks a patient a question about their health or a parent asks a child to repeat what they have said in an effort to make sense of what the child is trying to say.

Of course, when we do respond to what is written or said to us then we in turn can do so using language that is either written or spoken. And our spoken or written responses can in their turn be produced either with or without the expectation of a direct response.

What I have been doing here is to suggest that language use can be subcategorised in various ways. For example, one subcategory of language use is 'language use as spoken and as consumer'. Another is 'language use as spoken, and as producer, and with no response intended'. Yet another is 'language use as spoken, and as consumer, and with response required'. We can see that each subcategory of language use in effect makes some reference to some other or set of other subcategories. If we attempt to subcategorise the language use described for a day in my life this soon becomes clear.

For example, the radio news for me is language that I consume, that is, spoken and that requires no response. On the other hand, whilst the television news for me is also language that I consume, that is spoken and that requires no response, it can involve language that is both written and spoken.

An effective way of representing subcategories of something that are based on this sort of cross-referencing procedure is to use a diagram called a matrix. In the matrix below I have written labels for a few of the episodes of language use described for a day in my life across the page whilst I have written labels for types of language use down the side of the page. This then gives us a top-to-bottom column under each episode label and a side-to-side line extending to the right from each language-use label. Under each column we can now place the symbol '+'

	Listening to radio	Giving a lecture	Writing a memo	Reading a newspaper	Interviewing
Producer		+	+		+
Consumer	+			+	+
Written			+	+	+
Spoken	+	+			+
Response intended			+		+
Response required					+

against the appropriate language use if that particular type of language use applies to the episode in question.

Activity 1.3

Identify other language episodes described for a day in my life and construct a 'use matrix' for each of them. Remember that each matrix should be constructed from the perspective of me as the language user.

1.5 Language production and transmission – writing

Different cultures have evolved different ways of representing language in written form. Most involve visible marks of some kind on a flat surface, though others such as the braille system specifically developed for the blind can involve marks that are designed to be felt rather than seen.

The relationship of the written marks to the language represented can be of various kinds. Chinese, for example, uses what is called an ideographic system. This means that the written symbols used represent ideas that are directly expressed through the symbols rather than being linked to the sounds that would express the idea in the spoken language.

Japanese, on the other hand, combines the use of ideographic with syllabic symbols. This means that individual symbols are used to represent whole syllables rather than isolated sounds.

It is usually supposed that English uses an alphabetic system for its representation. This means that individual symbols are used to represent individual sounds of the spoken language rather than larger chunks such as the syllable. Of course, the situation is not quite as straightforward as this. Particular sounds can be represented by a wide range of different alphabetic letters and particular letters can represent a wide range of different sounds. In the following list you will see that the letters in bold type represent the same sound if the words are said out loud:

achi**e**ve rec**ei**ve s**ee**n sc**e**ne b**e**an

In the following list you will see that the letters in bold type, although the same, in fact represent quite different sounds:

Re**s**t re**s**ist revi**s**ion pen**s**ion

Furthermore it turns out that users of written English do indeed incorporate certain symbols that can be viewed as ideographic. For example, certain road signs such as the 'NO ENTRY' sign with its distinctive circle and horizontal bar are ideographic. Symbols such as '+', '_', '=', '&', '%', '$', can be routinely found in written texts and with each of them we immediately associate a particular idea or meaning rather than first constructing a spoken equivalent. These are then also ideographs. Symbols like '?' are used to indicate that what is written should be interpreted as having the function of a question. The symbol '!' is used to indicate that what is written should be interpreted as having the function of an exclamation or some sort of order. The symbols '...' are used to indicate that what is written is perhaps taken from some other discourse and so is explicitly signalled as having the special status of reported speech. And full stops, commas, colons etc. are used to signal a range of matters to do with how elements of grammatical structure or the writer's thoughts should be interpreted.

Whatever the marks used in writing they can be written with hand-held writing instruments such as pens, pieces of chalk and the like; typeset printing machines such as publishers of books, magazines and newspapers use; keyboards with a directly printed output such as typewriters; keyboards with a screen visual display such as word-processing systems; electronic mail and facsimile or fax machines that make instant written communication across the world possible.

1.6 Language production and transmission – speaking

Talk also makes use of a variety of audible gestures in the transmission of messages using language. Apart from the familiar individual segments of the sort that we have learned make up the word *c-a-t*, for example, there are the ways in which we can produce whispered voice, loud voice, whining voice, laughing voice, the voice going up, the voice going down, the voice going up and down, stress, pause, sighs, laughter, snorts etc., to help us put our messages into language. Furthermore, talk can be conducted almost entirely with the use of non-audible gestures as is the case with signing systems for the deaf or be heavily supplemented by such gestures as is the case for most face-to-face conversations and public speaking.

Whatever type or range of audible gesture used recent technological developments have also had an effect on how we speak to each other. Spoken messages can be produced and transmitted face to face for an audience of one or several consumers. Sometimes it can be the intention of the speaker that a consumer respond to what is said and sometimes this is not the intention. Spoken messages can also be produced and transmitted to an individual consumer who is distant in space via the telephone or radio. Indeed, there is now even the possibility of telephone conferencing involving many producers and consumers at the same time. Spoken messages can be recorded and then transmitted to an audience that is distant in time, i.e. to an audience that hears the message in the future. Massive and geographically distant audiences of non-responding consumers can be reached with messages transmitted via radio waves.

Activity 1.4 _____

Suggest reasons for selecting one means of production and transmission over others for the following types of message and consumers.

Message	Audience
A fairy story	A group of 5-year-olds
A love story	15 million teenagers of widely differing academic ability
A complaint about a product	A large department store
News of a relative's death	A sister in Australia

1.7 Situation, participants and purposes

Whether written or spoken, the language people use will be produced and adjusted in various ways according to what specific purposes they have, what particular people they are attempting to communicate with, in what capacity they see themselves as communicating, and what particular circumstances seem relevant at the time and in the situation the attempted communication is taking place.

Consider, for example, the episode I described earlier in which I found myself driving with my daughter to work with her at the wheel. In this episode I had the **given role** of father but the temporarily **assumed role** of driving instructor. In talking to my daughter in the capacity of driving instructor I assume my purposes would include instruction on what to do, when to do it, and how to do it with the overall aims of improving her driving skills and ensuring the safety of ourselves and other road users. All this talk would occur in particular circumstances, e.g. both of us sitting facing forward and not maintaining eye contact, both of us sitting in cramped conditions with a high level of engine noise, and each of us aware of the tension-induced irritability that had characterised previous episodes such as this one, occuring as it does early in the morning of a winter Monday.

It's easy to see how these facts can lead to adjustments in language use. The very fact that I am giving instructions, and that I am giving them to someone I have treated more or less as a child for almost 20 years, will mean that some sorts of grammatical structures are used more than others. What I say will be so formulated as to get mainly non-verbal responses from my daughter and in order to ensure our safety I will keep what I say brief and to the point. I am likely to say such things as *Turn left now* rather than the equivalent but grammatically more extended

The turning which will appear next to the left of our vehicle is the turning which I want you to take. When I refer to things outside the car I can make the assumption that both of us can see what is being referred to and this no doubt will affect the terms and structures I use to refer to things. I would no doubt choose to say *Mind that bloke* rather than *I'd just like to ask you to initiate an avoidance procedure so that the car doesn't make contact with the bicycle immediately in front being ridden by that adult male with the terrified look on his face.*

Engine and traffic noise will affect the loudness we choose to speak with. Whilst attempting to be brief and to the point previous experience of explosive moments of tension will mean that hastily given instructions will, whenever possible, have their potential brusqueness softened with other words, carefully chosen tones of voice and voice quality so as to minimise or avoid the giving of any possible offence.

Of course, not all the talk will be focused on the driving process and each of us may well slip in and out of different **speaker** and **listener roles**. One moment I might assume an 'advice-giving father' role as I respond to complaints about the tedium of school. The next moment I might slip into what we might call a 'concerned friend' listener role as my daughter relates a tale of tragedy and woe regarding the life of someone we both know. Such talk as this will inevitably exhibit a range of features different from those involved in the business of instructing someone to drive.

The following would be a useful checklist to determine major variations in the language likely to be used on any particular occasion:

(i) Are any special/technical/slang words likely?

(ii) Are any particular grammatical patterns such as interrogative sentences, passive sentences, long and complicated noun phrases, verb phrases or prepositional phrases likely?

(iii) Are long, short or varied-length speaking turns likely?

(iv) What sorts of things are the participants likely to do with their speaking turns – are they likely to ask questions, answer questions, seek clarification, make complaints, make requests, offer advice, offer sympathy, tell jokes or what?

(v) Who is likely to get the talk going and who is likely to bring it to a close?

(vi) How will the speakers use their voices – are they likely to be loud, emphatic or wheedling?

(vii) Is it likely that the participants will use a lot of non-verbal gesturing?

(viii) Is it likely that the talk will be fluent or is it likely that there will be much hesitation, repetition and the like?

Activity 1.5

A patient visits a doctor during normal surgery hours with severe and persistent stomach pains. Discuss how the participants' roles, their purposes and the circumstances of the situation might affect what is said, how it is said, and by whom.

Discussion

Your discussion of the doctor/patient consultation will obviously have been shaped to some extent by your own background and personal history of encounters with doctors and even by your encounters with fictional representations of such encounters in books, theatre or films. Most of us, though, tend to think in terms of stereotypes when we think about the behaviour of categories of person in particular situations. One might say that we have in mind what amounts to a sort of *script* which we share with others and which shapes and guides behaviour. That is, most of us have similar ideas about what the typical doctor does when talking to a typical patient about a typical problem.

In our society, for example, doctors are usually accorded a superior status in situations of professional consultation such as the one under consideration. (We might contrast this with the status accorded the refuse collector when he is consulted in his professional capacity.) This might well mean that a doctor will express this routinely assumed superiority in the way his questions are formulated. For example, is the doctor more likely to put a question in the form *Tell me how many times you go to the lavatory each day* or in the form *I don't suppose you'd care to tell me how many times you go to the lavatory each day?*

Patients might well in their turn express recognition and/or acceptance of the assumed superiority by, for example, only speaking when asked a direct question.

The question of roles might be further complicated if we consider the sex of either the patient or the doctor. Consultations with doctors can involve very intimate physical examination and we might expect that talk accompanying such examination will reflect and be sensitive to the sex of both doctor and patient. Again we might expect the degree of acquaintance between the two participants to have some bearing on how talk is produced during what is essentially a professional encounter. For example is a male doctor more likely in the course of examining a female patient to say *Take your knickers off, I want to look at your backside* or *Just remove your lower clothing, I need to take a quick look down there*?

The doctor will have as a primary aim or purpose the discovery of what might be the cause of the symptoms being presented by the patient and this will inevitably involve the doctor in asking a series of questions sequenced in such a way as to systematically rule out certain possibilities whilst focusing in on others.

Because bodily pain is involved the patient will need to integrate quite elaborate physical gesturing with any talk that is produced. No one but the patient can experience the pain so we can expect much subjective and often metaphorical uses of language as the patient attempts indirectly to share the experience of particular pain with references to short, sharp, stabbing, or perhaps just throbbing pains.

The doctor, of course, will be under enormous pressure to see as many patients as possible during the hours of surgery and so we can expect the whole episode to be characterised by a sense of getting through the business as quickly as possible. This will have an effect on the overall control of the whole episode with the doctor producing talk that is more or less precisely designed to maintain that control.

Activity 1.6

A motorist stops to ask a passing pedestrian for directions. Discuss how the participants' roles, their purposes and the circumstances of the situation might affect what is said, how it is said, and by whom.

2. Imagining the organisation of talk

2.1 Introduction

In the last chapter we made use of our everyday commonsense knowledge of people's everyday lives as a basis for our preliminary investigations of language use. In particular we used such knowledge to build up a picture of how situation, participants and purposes can shape the language that might be used in the course of particular episodes in the lives of ordinary people going about their ordinary business. The episodes we looked at in most detail involved **spoken verbal interaction**.

In spoken verbal interaction people use their voices to communicate with one another. They use their voices to articulate words that are put together into sequences according to the rules of the language being spoken. When people engaging in spoken verbal interaction say things, they do so with the intention that the person they are trying to communicate with respond to what has been said in similar ways. Moreover, they also intend that there be some response. It will be just those sorts of episode where spoken verbal interaction occurs that we shall be investigating in what follows.

Activity 2.1

Identify which of the following are examples of spoken verbal interaction:

Reading the six o'clock news
Sending an SOS via morse code
Making a telephone call
Speaking to an answer machine
Writing a memo or letter
Using a dictaphone
Saying a prayer
Using a one-way radio
Yodelling
Using semaphore
Using British Sign Language (BSL)
Acting in *Hamlet*
Role-playing in a French lesson
Using electronic mail (E-mail)
Making a speech in the House of Commons
Making a speech as part of a Party Political Broadcast

Discussion

I would suggest that the following are clear examples of spoken verbal interaction because each involves the use of words articulated with the voice and spoken with the intention that there be some specific response:

> *Making a telephone call*
> *Role-playing in a French lesson*

I would suggest that the following are clearly not examples of spoken verbal interaction because in some cases words are articulated with the voice but there can be no intention that there be some response, or at least no immediate response, that is similarly articulated, e.g. *Reading the six o'clock news*; in some cases words are articulated with the intention that there be some sort of response but some means other than the voice is used, e.g. *Using British Sign Language (BSL)*; and in some cases there is communication with the intention that there be some response but no words are articulated, e.g. *Yodelling*.

> *Reading the six o'clock news*
> *Sending an SOS via morse code*
> *Speaking to an answer machine*
> *Writing a memo or letter*
> *Using a dictaphone*
> *Using a one-way radio*

Yodelling
Using semaphore
Using British Sign Language (BSL)
Using electronic mail (E-mail)
Making a speech as part of a Party Political Broadcast

I would suggest that it is a matter for debate whether the following are examples of spoken verbal interaction because in the first case it would have to be agreed that God actually speaks directly to those who pray; in the second case the idea of there being some intended response perhaps does not arise because whatever can be said is completely determined by the text of the play and has nothing to do with the intentions of the actors; and in the third case whilst Members of Parliament can indeed be interrupted with responses to what they have to say it seems unlikely at least that it is ever part of their intentions that they be so interrupted.

Saying a prayer
Acting in Hamlet
Making a speech in the House of Commons

2.2 Spoken verbal interaction

The focus of our investigations, then, will be the kind of language use that involves people as people who, during the course of the same episode, both consume spoken language and produce it. We can note immediately that such language will have the following characteristics:

(i)   it is for the most part not subject to prior conscious detailed planning;

(ii) it is produced with the intention that the consumer of it actually respond in some more or less specific way;

(iii) responses to such language will be produced in similar ways and with similar expectations of response;

(iv) it will be shaped on a moment-by-moment basis by the roles the individuals have or take on, by the purposes they have, and by the situation in which the talk takes place.

Each of the following activities should help confirm for you in what ways spoken verbal interaction does indeed have these characteristics.

Characteristic (i): lack of conscious detailed planning

Activity 2.2

Compare the following sorts of talk and decide to what extent they might be subject to prior conscious detailed planning:

(a)   A radio news broadcast
(b)   A comedian telling a joke/story
(c)   A commentator describing a major royal occasion
(d)   A television interview with the Prime Minister
(e)   An interview on a television chat show
(f)   A telephone salesperson selling double-glazing
(g)   A marriage proposal
(h)   A commentator describing a football match
(i)   A teacher teaching a class
(j)   A job interview
(k)   An argument between two friends
(l)   A chat amongst friends in a café

Characteristic (ii): expectation of response

When a question is asked the person who has been asked the question (the consumer) is usually expected to respond with an answer. The following are examples of pairs of questions and answers:

→ *A*   Who are you?
　 B   John.
→ *A*   What are you writing?
　 B   A book.
→ *A*   When will you finish?
　 B   Next month.
→ *A*   Why don't you use a word-processor?
　 B   Because I can't afford it.
→ *A*   How much will it cost?
　 B   Ten pounds.
→ *A*   Will it be in paperback?
　 B   No.
→ *A*   It'll be in the shops by July, will it?
　 B   Yes.

Notice how the way in which these questions are put together or **formulated** forces any next speaker to respond with something that is recognisable as an answer to the question asked and indeed, to some extent, the **formulation** can force the answer itself to be formulated in a particular way.

We can do other things in talk that set up expectations of specific sorts of response. When we complain to someone about their behaviour, for example, it is usual to expect that the person will produce an apology, a justification, an excuse or some combination of these expected responses. Where doing one thing with an utterance in talk sets up the expectation of a particular sort of thing being done in response, or at least where it makes the doing of the thing highly relevant, we can speak of paired utterances or **adjacency pairs**.

The first speaker's utterance is the **first pair part** and the second speaker's utterance is the **second pair part**.

Activity 2.3 _____

(a) Discuss what things should be done as expected responses when someone produces:

a request	some good news
an accusation	a joke
a compliment	a greeting
some bad news	a comment on the weather

(b) Construct an imaginary dialogue for each item.

Characteristic (iii): responses designed to be responses and also to elicit further response

Activity 2.4 _____

Identify which speaker's turns in the following constructed dialogue are:

(a) trying to get a response from the other person or
(b) actually providing a response or
(c) both trying to get a response and to provide one.

$\rightarrow$ *A* What time do you think they'll arrive?
   B I was hoping you would tell me.

> *A* Well you're the one who saw them last.
> *B* So that makes me an expert on their intentions I suppose.
> *A* You do speak to them, don't you?
> *B* And you don't?
> *A* There are some things you just can't mention to them or hadn't you noticed?
> *B* Exactly!
> *etc., etc., etc.*

For each speaker's turn identify what it might be about it that shows it is either a response or expects a response.

Example 1

> → *B* I was hoping you would tell me.

Taken out of the context of where this occurs in the conversation it would be difficult to make sense of this – what, we might wonder, is it that the speaker is hoping he or she might be told. The answer to this question, of course, is *when they will arrive*. B's speaking turn could, then, be seen as an incomplete or **elliptical** sentence. The bit that makes it incomplete can be recovered from the context; in this case the crucial context is the immediately preceding speaking turn. It's as if the speaker is to be understood to be saying:

> → *B* I was hoping you would tell me (when they will arrive).

with the bit in brackets to be taken as understood on the basis that the sentence is a response to a question that contains the relevant information. So here the very fact that the speaking turn makes use of an elliptical sentence shows it is some sort of response.

Example 2

> → *B* So that makes me an expert on their intentions I suppose.

A crucial clue here to the fact that this is produced as a response is the use of the word *so* right at the beginning of the speaking turn. The word *so* is a linking word used to link ideas, often within a sentence. The following is such a use:

<I saw them last so that makes me an expert on their intentions.>

Here the fact that I saw them last is linked, through the use of the word *so*, to the fact of my expertise on their intentions. But in the case of B's speaking turn there simply is nothing said in the turn that the word *so* provides a link for. Partly this is because the word occurs at the beginning of the speaking turn so the link that is provided for must be to something said in some earlier speaking turn. It is because this is the only way in which the word *so* can be interpreted here that it shows that the speaking turn which its use initiates is to be heard as some sort of response.

Characteristic (iv): what things get said, and how, is a matter of who, what, where, when, and why

Activity 2.5

The following sorts of things are often said in the course of conversation and, furthermore, are often said in a variety of ways:

→ Don't be catty.
→ Listen, pal, I'm telling you, not asking you. OK?
→ I hardly think this is the right time or the right place.

(a) Discuss the sorts of thing that might have led to these things being said in particular conversations (pay particular attention to vocabulary that might be more usually used by or applied to males or females).

Examples

→ Don't be catty.

Someone, probably female, is criticising a person who turns out to be a friend of the person they are speaking to.

→ Listen, pal, I'm telling you, not asking you. OK?

Someone, probably male, has already hinted that an uninvited guest, again probably male, leave a party. The hint has not been taken.

→ I hardly think this is the right time or the right place.

Someone has just started to tell a funny story at a funeral.

(b) Discuss the relationships that the people saying these things to each other in this way might have.

(c) Suggest other ways of saying the same things and comment on what sorts of relationships would go with these different ways of saying things.

Examples:
→ It's not always easy to judge why people do things.
→ Look I've tried to do this in as civil a way as possible, but now I really must insist that you leave.
→ Is that the vicar coming over.

2.3 From guesses to observations to descriptions to discoveries

In investigating spoken verbal interaction we shall need to go beyond the picture-building sort of approach based on intuition that we have adopted so far. This has simply been a matter of more or less informed guesses about who **might** say what to whom, and how what **might** be said **might** actually get said. These guesses or **hypotheses** might well give us ideas about what to look for when investigating spoken verbal interaction. But as mere guesses or hypotheses they need to be confirmed by detailed and careful observation of actual instances of people talking to one another. Only if we can confirm our hypotheses can we properly be said to have **knowledge** about what really goes on.

In order to demonstrate this approach to finding things out we shall focus on a rather minute detail of just one aspect of spoken verbal interaction, i.e. a detail of pronunciation. We shall look at the pronunciation of what is probably one of the most commonly occurring words in the English language. We shall in fact be looking in some detail at the pronunciation of the word *the*. It is fairly common knowledge that the pronunciation of this word can be variable. Sometimes it is pronounced in a way that for the moment might be most effectively represented as *thuh* and sometimes it is pronounced in a way that might be represented as *thee*. The question is – do speakers use these pronunciations at random or are they in some way systematic in selecting one rather than the other when they engage in spoken verbal interaction?

To begin to answer this question let's look at how we would pronounce the word as it occurs in the last sentence of the immediately preceding paragraph. Read the sentence out loud and ask someone to listen carefully to your pronunciation of the word each time it occurs.

The word actually occurs twice – right at the beginning in the noun phrase *the question* and towards the end in the noun phrase *the other*. You will most probably find that for the first noun phrase you pronounced *the* as *thuh* whilst for the second noun phrase you pronounced it as *thee*.

Activity 2.6

Consider your pronunciation of the word the if you were to use it before the following nouns:

book, apron, cat, dog, frog, apple, girl, house, job, end, offer, kite, lamp, man, note, orchard, umbrella, pan, rat, safe, town, van, ink, wall, youth, arrest, arm, eye, zoo, shriek, owl, church, earth, oil, overture, thrush

Discussion

You should have found that your pronunciations were sometimes with the *thuh* variant and sometimes with the *thee* variant.

Now list the nouns under each variant. What you should find is that those nouns listed under the *thuh* variant all begin with a consonant whilst those listed under the *thee* variant all begin with a vowel. This would indicate that when people are carefully reading lists of words their pronunciation of *the* is quite precisely affected by the context in which it occurs. Specifically, pronunciation of *the* is affected by whether it precedes a vowel or a consonant. We have some basis then for **hypothesising** that in spoken verbal interaction the use of *thuh* or *thee* is not random but rather depends on the context in which the word occurs.

However, our evidence so far is drawn from a very specialised use of language, i.e. the careful reading out loud of something that is written down. To confirm that our hypothesis holds for spoken verbal interaction we must listen to people actually talking to one another.

Activity 2.7

Tape-record a group of up to five people talking to one another. It is best if you choose a room which is carpeted so that echo and other noise is reduced. For this exercise the recorder could be placed in the middle of the group and the people given a subject to discuss. Play back your recording and note how each instance of 'the' is pronounced, paying close attention to the word that immediately follows.

Discussion

You should have found that whilst *thuh* and *thee* are mostly pronounced in the ways predicted, i.e. *thuh* before consonants and *thee* before vowels, it does happen that *thee* sometimes occurs before a word that begins with a consonant. However, with very careful listening to your recording you should find that the *thee* pronunciation does not *immediately* precede the words beginning with a consonant. Rather you will find the typical marks of non-fluency in speech – *erms*, *ers* pauses and the like intervening between the word *the* and the following word beginning with a consonant.

So we find *thee* being used, not because the speaker knows there is an immediately following word that begins with a vowel, but rather because the speaker knows that there is an immediately following hitch in the flow of talk that the speaker may choose to fill with a sound, not a word, that begins with a vowel. The hypothesis as formulated is therefore not confirmed.

We need, in effect, to 'refine' or 'fine-tune' the hypothesis because the contexts which affect the pronunciation of *the* need to be more precisely specified than they were in the original. Speakers, it turns out, do routinely use *thee* before words beginning with consonants: they do this, it seems, when there is to be a subconsciously planned-for hitch in the talk.

But the fact that the original hypothesis is not confirmed should lead us to think differently about *erms*, *ers*, pauses and the like as they occur in people's speech. Our refined hypothesis can lead us to think of such phenomena not just as random occurrences interrupting the normally fluent flow of talk but as subconsciously planned for on a moment-by-moment basis. So from one hypothesis that turns out not to be confirmed we can actually formulate a new hypothesis as a result of what our investigation of the first showed us.

This exercise concerning the pronunciation of the most-used word in the language highlights two crucial issues for us as we approach the investigation of spoken verbal interaction. Firstly, it underlines the need to confirm our hypotheses about how we talk to one another by careful observation of instances of actually occurring talk. Secondly, it demonstrates that no detail of people's behaviour should be overlooked when they are talking if an accurate description of what is happening is to be arrived at. Here, for example, we saw how apparent non-fluencies in speech can affect aspects of pronunciation and so in fact be seen to be in some way under the control of the speaker. In effect the exercise demonstrates that some non-fluencies, far from being sudden failures in the smooth flow of talk, can be and actually are planned for.

Activity 2.8

When one speaker wants to show another speaker that what they have said was not clear in some way then one thing they can do to remedy the situation is to say *Pardon?*. It would seem a reasonable hypothesis to suggest that the person to whom *Pardon?* is addressed will respond with a repetition of the queried utterance. Query what people say with *Pardon?* and assess the extent to which the hypothesis is confirmed. (Note what happens in at least 15 instances.)

You will almost certainly have found as a result of the last activity that people hardly ever respond to *pardons* with a straightforward repetition of what was originally said. Remember that an exact repetition of something said would require identity of tone of voice as well as identity of the words and grammar used. Identity of tone of voice is hardly ever achieved but apart from this you will have found that more often than not people change the words and grammar of what was said.

Again then we can see that what at first seems an entirely plausible hypothesis turns out on the basis of careful observation not to be confirmed. And the fact that it is not confirmed should lead us to reconsider how we think about what is going on when people use a word like *pardon*. We might well have thought, for example, that the use of *pardon* signals that the person using it considers him/herself to be at fault in the interaction. Surely *pardon* is used as a way of showing that insufficient attention was being paid by a listener and, as a result of that, something that should have been heard was not heard. The implied remedy, then, is for the speaker to repeat what was said. But the fact that speakers often don't produce repetitions in response to *pardons* suggests that they are behaving as if something quite different is going on in the interaction. One possibility is that they feel it is they and not the person producing the *pardon* who has been at fault. They feel, perhaps, that they have produced an utterance which is in some way flawed and which therefore must be changed – hence the lack of straightforward repetition.

Activity 2.9 _____

The expression *OK* often occurs when people talk to one another. We might hypothesise that when it is used it is to express the idea that something is in order or acceptable. Listen to the use of OK in people's talk, decide what meaning or meanings it is actually used to convey and discuss whether your observations confirm the hypothesis.

Discussion

The following are some of the contexts in which I have heard, recorded and transcribed the expression *OK*:

> → *A* These are OK.
> → *A* These are OK people.

In these cases the expression is used as if it were an adjective with something like the meanings *in order* or *definitely acceptable*.

> → *A* Can you give this the OK?

In this case the expression is used as a noun with something like the meanings *the status of being in order* or *the status of being acceptable*.

> → *A* You can OK this, can't you?

In this case the expression is used as a verb with something like the meanings *accord the status of being in order* or *accord the status of being acceptable*.

You will have noticed that for each of these examples the meanings are more or less as hypothesised. But in each case I have used a grammatical term to categorise the expression and corresponding to each different category there is a very slight difference of meaning. I have called the expression an adjective, a noun and a verb. There is nothing in the make-up of the expression itself which has enabled me to make these categorisations. Rather I have made the categorisations on the basis of where the expression occurs in the sequence of words. So, for example, we expect expressions which come immediately before words like *people* in a sequence to be adjectives, e.g. *nice people, good people, white people, fat people.* Similarly, we expect expressions which come after words like *the* in a sequence such as *the boy, the girl, the fruit, the truth* to be nouns. And finally we expect expressions that come immediately after words like *can* in a sequence to be verbs, e.g. *can come, can go, can sing, can run.* Differences of meaning would thus seem to correspond to differences in **sequential position**.

Now let's look at a further set of examples of the use of *OK* where it doesn't seem quite right to use categories like adjective, noun or verb but where, as we shall see, the expressions have distinct meanings and those meanings can be related to where they occur in a sequence. But this time we shall need to make reference to sequences of speaking turns rather than simply sequences of words.

> → *A* Can I have a chocolate?
> → *B* OK.

In this case the expression is in effect a whole speaking turn and is a response to a request with something like the meaning *Yes you can have a chocolate.*

> → *A* OK, let's move on to the next topic.

In this case the expression is a part of a speaking turn, though not in any sense a part of a sentence, and is used as a way of marking a sort of break in the talk with something like the meaning *At this point there is a break with what has gone before and what follows is to be treated as separate from it.*

> → *A* Don't do that, OK?
> → *B* OK.

In this case the expression as used by A is again a part of a speaking turn but not in any sense a part of a sentence. Here the expression seems to be being used as a way of getting the speaker B to respond with a confirmation and has a meaning something like *say yes*. B, on the other hand, uses the expression as a complete speaking turn with the meaning *Yes*.

<pre>
      A   So see you Monday.
 →   B   OK.
 →   A   OK.
      B   Bye.
      A   Bye.
</pre>

In this case B's *OK* would seem to be used as a way of showing agreement whilst A's *OK* is at the very least an acknowledgement of that agreement, though as we shall see it could be more besides. But in each case our understanding of the meanings of the expression goes beyond the meanings hypothesised and is based on the sequential positions of the expression within speaking turns or series of speaking turns.

It is clear, then, that in order to achieve an accurate description of episodes of social behaviour involving spoken verbal interaction we need to go beyond simple speculation about what may or may not be the case. We need accurate records of actual interactions. Video and audio recording now enable us to make cheap, good quality records. However, to make the detailed and careful observations necessary for an adequate description of spoken verbal interaction it has proved essential to make written transcriptions of what is said so that the process of interaction can be 'frozen' and then subjected to precise and careful observation. The next chapter shows how written transcriptions of what is said can be made so as to provide enough detail for an investigator to build up a detailed and accurate picture of what is actually going on in any instance of spoken verbal interaction.

Activity 2.10

Investigate the hypothesis that when people talk to one another they speak in sentences whenever they get a turn at speaking.

3. Transcribing the organisation of talk

3.1 Introduction

The episodes of spoken verbal interaction that we shall be investigating will be ones in which the talk has a central, rather than a peripheral, role in the interaction. To investigate such episodes in any detail we must first make recordings of what has been said.

3.2 Slowing speech down

Anyone who has played 'Chinese whispers', where a whispered message is successively passed from person to person, will have seen just how distorted messages can become, even in short-term memory. Audio or video recordings thus provide the opportunity of endlessly replaying the whole, or segments, of some interactional episode that we might want to investigate.

But endlessly replaying some episode will not necessarily give us greater insight into what is going on. A first problem is that things happen very quickly and no sooner is something said than our attention switches to what a speaker is going on to say. There is simply no time to focus on details. A second major difficulty is that it is not at all easy when listening to talk not to listen to it as someone involved in the talk, i.e. as someone whose main concern is to make sense of what is being said. It is rather more difficult to focus on just those details of what is said that may or may not happen to contribute to its sense.

Consider, for example, the difficulty you would have in reporting on the details of the letter and word shapes of this sentence which might contribute to how you make sense of it as you read it. Do you read the words as wholes or do you take in just parts of words – individual letters or letter combinations? If it's just the parts of words that you are taking in is it the whole of a letter shape that's important or just a part of the letter shape? If it's part of a letter shape then which part is important – top, bottom or what?

We therefore need to transform the talk we want to investigate into a form that provides us with the equivalent of a 'freeze-frame'. Such a 'freeze-frame' of talk would enable us to inspect it whilst it is, as it were, not moving. The 'freeze-frame' also needs to be in a form that makes available for inspection all those details which might contribute to its sense. These would include details that we tend to edit out, or don't consciously attend to, when listening to talk, as we normally do, just for its sense. We can achieve this necessary transformation of talk into a 'freeze-frame' by converting it into written form or into the form of a **transcription**.

3.3 Choosing a set of symbols

Of course, the alphabetic writing system of standard orthography that I am using to write this was originally a system for transcribing the spoken medium. If you inspect English texts written some centuries ago, for example, you will find different spellings of the same word reflecting the different attempts of individual writers to represent in writing their own ways of pronouncing things.

But even given the standardisation of the English spelling system writers have continued to manipulate spelling conventions in order to signal to their readers some peculiarity or other in the speech that is being represented. This can be done for a variety of reasons – to enhance characterisation, for humorous effect or to facilitate research of the details of what has been said.

Activity 3.1

Following are some examples of individual writers' attempts to represent the actual pronunciation of the speech of their characters.

(i) Attempt to 'hear' the talk in the way you assume the writers intended and check to see if your 'hearings' are similar to those of others in your group.

(ii) Work out the conventions the writers would seem to be using so as to make the talk 'hearable' in the way intended.

(iii) Comment on the consistency with which the conventions are used.

1. Sam Weller giving advice to his son Samuel (Charles Dickens, *Pickwick Papers* (Oxford University Press, 1961))

> 'I'm a goin' to leave you, Samivel my boy, and there's no telling ven I shall see you again. Your mother-in-law may ha' been too much for me, or a thousand things may have happened by the time you next hears any news o' the the celebrated Mr Veller o' the Bell Savage. The family name depends wery much on you, Samivel, and I hope you'll do wot's right by it. Upon all little pints o' breedin', I know I may trust you as vell as if it was my own self. So I've only this here one little piece of adwice to give you. If ever you gets to up'ards o' fifty, and feels disposed to go a marryin' anybody – no matter who – jist you shut yourself up in your own room, if you've got one, and pison yourself off hand. Hangin's wulgar, so don't you have nothin' to say to that. Pison yourself, Samivel, my boy, pison yourself, and you'll be glad on it arterwards.'

2. Mr Morel accounts for his time at the pub to Mrs Morel (D. H. Lawrence, *Sons and Lovers* (Heinemann, 1972))

> 'Oh! Oh! waitin' for me, lass? I've bin 'elpin' Anthony an' what's think he's gen me? Nowt b'r a lousy hae'f-crown, an' that's ivry penny –'
> 'He thinks you've made the rest up in beer,' she said shortly.
> 'An' I 'aven't – that I 'aven't. You b'lieve me, I've 'ad very little this day, I have an' all.' His voice went

tender. 'Here, an' I browt thee a bit o' brandysnap, an' a cocoanut for th' children.' He laid the ginger-bread and the cocoanut, a hairy object, on the table. 'Nay, tha niver said thankyer for nowt i' thy life, did ter?'

As a compromise, she picked up the cocoanut and shook it, to see if it had any milk.

'It's a good 'un, you can back yer life o' that. I got it fra' Bill Hodgkisson. "Bill," I says, "tha non wants them three nuts, does ter? Arena ter for gi'ein' me one for my bit of a lad an' wench?" "I ham, Walter, my lad," 'e says; "ta'e which on 'em ter's a mind." An' so I took one, an' thanked 'im. I didn't like ter shake it afore 'is eyes, but 'e says, "Tha'd better ma'e sure it's a good un, Walt." An' so, yer see, I knowed it was. He's a nice chap, is Bill Hodgkisson, 'e's a nice chap!'

'A man will part with anything so long as he's drunk, and you're drunk along with him,' said Mrs Morel.

'Eh, tha mucky little 'ussy, who's drunk, I sh'd like ter know?' said Morel.

3. The colonel and his friend (Afferbeck Lauder, *Fraffly Suite*)

Demmertol Mogret, chep zirnia winker monda. Snort ziffy was an F.I. Smoshel. Feller rotterby cot mo-shelled. Gairdwee do things bettrin the yommy. Arrer member beckon 47, or meffpin 48. Any wet was in Tripoli. No, meffpin nelleck-zendri-yaw.

Earce. Ears of coss. End now, meddier Colonel, prep shoot lacquer little something tweet. Eddu wishooed trair little sneck. Arm shawr chewler gree wimmer steffer nother little toxoon. Shuggah?

4. E invites N to lunch cited in P. Drew, 'Speakers' Reportings in Invitation Sequences', in J. M. Atkinson and J. Heritage (eds), *Structures of Social Action* (Cambridge University Press, 1984))

E   Wanna cum down'n av a bighta lunch with me?
     I got s'm beer en stuff
N   Wul yer ril sweet hon

E   or d'yuh'av sum p'n else t'

N   No I haf to call Rol's mother. I told'er I'd call 'er
      this morning I gotta letter from 'er en An'dum So
      in the letter she sed if you can why yih know call
      me Saturdih morning en I jist haven't
      T's like takin' a beating

Discussion

Whilst it's likely that there will have been some points of
agreement as to how the talk should have been heard, it's
unlikely that there will have been full agreement. For example,
we find regular substitutions in the Dickens piece of *v* for *w* as in
Weller, of *w* for *v* as in *very*, and *i* for the vowel sound *oi* as in
point. Everyone should be able to 'hear' these items as intended.
But we should also note the inconsistency with which this convention is applied in the way the words *one*, *every* and *boy* are
represented.

Nevertheless, in the cases of the Dickens and Lawrence ex-
tracts it's likely that the most successful 'hearings' would be by
those of you who know the writers and the particular novels.
There would then have been strong expectations of London and
Nottingham pronunciations. But these expectations would aid
reconstruction of the intended 'hearings' only to the extent that
the reader was familiar with typical London and Nottingham
speech.

The content of the *Fraffly Suite* extract would have suggested
the pronunciation typical of a small subgroup of the English
upper class, but again reconstruction would be possible only to
the extent that the pronunciation of that particular subgroup was
familiar.

A mutually agreed 'hearing' for the lunch invitation extract is
much more difficult to reconstruct because no contextual cues
are provided. However, this is a transcription of tape-recorded
speech made for the purposes of research into what details of
talk matter in interaction. The transcription is therefore not
primarily intended for readers other than the researcher. Rather,
it is intended as a reminder to the researcher of their particular
'hearing' of what was said. Repeated and detailed listening to the
actual recording on which the transcription is based is the

researcher's basis for how to interpret and therefore 'hear' the transcription.

These highly individual phoneticised representations of speech would then seem to have their intended effect on the reader only if the reader has some additional means of knowing what sort of pronunciation is being suggested. Thus we can read the pieces and 'hear' as intended only if we already know what 'hearing' is intended.

3.4 Beyond the words

There is much that we hear in the stream of speech in addition to the sounds by which we recognise the individual words. Punctuation marks such as capital letters, full stops, question marks, commas etc., were introduced to go some way to represent the pauses, rhythms and tunes that are such a feature of the way people talk.

Activity 3.2 _____

Read the following speech taken from Shakespeare's *Henry V*. The speech is clearly intended as a stirring pep talk from the English king to his troops before they enter battle.

I have written out the speech without any punctuation. You will find that this makes reading the speech for performance, in a way that was probably intended, very difficult. You have to make decisions about what groups of words belong together, when to make long pauses, when to make short pauses, when to adopt a querying tone of voice, when to adopt a tone that indicates you are stating the obvious, when to raise your voice etc., etc.

Sort out in your own mind how you would expect the speech to be spoken and then use capital letters, commas, full stops, question marks, etc. to indicate the performance decisions you have made.

King Henry   once more unto the breach dear friends once more
or close the wall up with our english dead in peace
theres nothing so becomes a man as modest still-
ness and humility but when the blast of war blows
in our ears then imitate the action of the tiger
stiffen the sinews conjure up the blood disguise fair
nature with hard favoured rage then lend the eye a

terrible aspect let it pry through the portage of the head like the brass cannon let the brow overwhelm it as fearfully as doth a galled rock overhang and jutty his confounded base swilled with the wild and wasteful ocean now set the teeth and stretch the nostril wide hold hard the breath and bend up every spirit to his full height on on you noblest english whose blood is fet from fathers of war-proof fathers that like so many alexanders have in these parts from morn till even fought and sheathed their swords for lack of argument dishonour not your mothers now attest that those whom you called fathers did beget you be copy now to men of grosser blood and teach them how to war and you good yeomen whose limbs were made in england show us here the mettle of your pasture let us swear that you are worth your breeding which i doubt not for there is none of you so mean and base that hath not noble lustre in your eyes i see you stand like greyhounds in the slips straining upon the start the games afoot follow your spirit and upon this charge cry god for harry england and saint george

Discussion

One of the difficulties you will have encountered in trying to organise this speech through the use of punctuation is that it is not always obvious that you are dealing with sentences. And, of course, it is for sentences that we use the most common marks of punctuation such as the full stop or question mark. Even when it is fairly obvious that you are dealing with a sentence-like unit a further difficulty is to decide how it is being used. Is it being used to ask a question, make a statement or give an order? Once these decisions are made and marked with appropriate punctuation this will be of some use to other readers of the speech. But the usefulness is ultimately quite limited if the aim is to represent the patterns of stress, the rhythms, the tunes and the qualities of voice with which you think the speech should be performed. It is no accident that generations of actors have come up with widely differing performances of Shakespeare's speeches.

The speech just considered was, of course, written to be performed. Not all that is written is written with this intention – even when what is written is supposed to be a record of speech. Such is the case with the representations of characters' talk in novels where the reader is expected to reconstruct though not perform that talk.

Activity 3.3

Select a chapter from a novel containing a lot of dialogue and see what means the writer uses when reporting speech to indicate how what was said by the characters was actually said.

It might be useful to draw up two lists – one for the different words of 'saying' used by the author, e.g. *cried, murmured, whispered, laughed, insisted, gasped, sighed, shouted, whimpered, drawled, pouted* etc., and one for the descriptions of how things were said, e.g. *grumpily, hesitantly, brusquely, slowly, quickly, huskily, emphatically, with a smile, with a laugh, through his sobs, in measured tones*, etc.

Activity 3.4

For each of your two lists decide which of the items focus primarily on the physical characteristics of what you hear and which focus on other matters such as the social, psychological or conversational context of what is said. For example:

'I love you,' **whispered** the doctor.

= focus on physical.

'I love you,' **pouted** the doctor.

= focus on both physical (rounding and protrusion of lips) and social/psychological (we are led to assume that the doctor is female and possibly that the relationship of speaker to audience is of a sexual kind).

'I love you,' **replied** the doctor.

= focus on conversational context (we are led to believe that what the doctor says occurs at a particular sequential position in the conversation, i.e. following something another speaker has said).

Activity 3.5

Working in pairs demonstrate to each other how you would expect the following to have been said according to the three verbs of saying:

'Why don't you come up to my place sometime,' she **snapped/drawled/whimpered.**

Activity 3.6

Comment on what changes you and your partner have to make in the way the sentence is said. Think in particular about the speed at which the sentence needed to be said, whether certain words or parts of words needed to be emphasised with loudness or elongation and whether the voice needed to go particularly high or low.

Activity 3.7

The following is an extract from Nora Ephron's novel *Heartburn*. The extract is in fact just a part of a telephone conversation which the character Betty has made to Rachel and in which Rachel takes the opportunity to start a rumour about Thelma whom she suspects her own husband of having an affair with. Betty is unaware of Rachel's suspicion.

You will see that the author mostly uses the verb say in reporting the speech of the characters. Substitute alternative verbs of saying, or descriptions of ways of saying, to indicate how you think the things might have been said.

Heartburn – an extract

'Anyway, it doesn't matter,' said Betty, 'because I found out who Thelma Rice is having the affair with.'
'Who?' I said.
'You're not going to like it,' said Betty.
'Who is it?' I said.
'Arthur,' said Betty.
'Arthur Siegel?' I said.
'Yes,' said Betty. 'They were having drinks in the Washington Hilton yesterday afternoon. Nobody has drinks in the Washington Hilton unless something secret's going on.'

'Arthur isn't having an affair with Thelma Rice,' I said. 'Nobody is having an affair with Thelma Rice.'
'How do you know?' said Betty.
'I just know,' I said.
'Tell me,' said Betty.
'Okay,' I said, 'but you can't tell this to anyone.'
'I promise,' said Betty.
'I saw Thelma at the gynecologist's,' I lied, 'and that's when I found out.'
'What?' said Betty.
'She has this horrible infection,' I went on. 'You don't even want to know about it.'
'Oh, God,' said Betty.
'She made me promise not to tell anyone,' I said, 'but she almost didn't have to because it's so disgusting I almost couldn't. I'm only telling you because I want you to know it's not true about her and Arthur.'
'Then why was she having a drink with him?' said Betty.
'That's part of it,' I said.
'What are you talking about?' said Betty.
'She wanted some legal advice,' I said. 'She got the infection in a Vietnamese restaurant in Virginia, and she wants to sue them.'
'She got it from something she ate, or from the toilet seat?' said Betty.
'The toilet seat, I guess,' I said, 'although I'm not sure. Maybe from the spring rolls.'
'Oh, God,' said Betty. 'Poor Thelma.'
'Poor Thelma?' I said.
'I feel so sorry for her,' said Betty.
'Don't feel too sorry for her,' I said. 'It's curable. Eventually.'

(Nora Ephron, *Heartburn* (Pan Books, 1986) pp. 107–9)

Activity 3.8

Now compare your revised text with the transcribed extract from the film version of the book (see page 56). In the film the conversation is face to face and takes place during a chance encounter in a supermarket. Those with access to the film version will be able to compare the actors' performances with their own choice of verbs of saying etc.

What you have been exploring through the last three exercises are the many and subtle ways in which speakers can use their voices in order to say things in different ways. Some people are, of course, better than others at doing this. We can refer to an individual's ability to use their voice in these ways as the individual's **vocal repertoire**.

As you will have seen there are many aspects of vocal repertoire that the punctuation conventions for written texts simply cannot capture. Novelists overcome the problem of representing the vocal repertoires used by their characters by making use of a wide range of verbs and descriptions of 'saying' in addition to punctuation.

Punctuation of written texts is, of course, primarily concerned with organising the text in a way that is most easily understandable to a reader. The details of past or possible future performance are mostly of interest only to the extent that they might assist this process. And the descriptive terms for reported speech often have as much or more to do with interpretation of what is said as with the physical details of how it is said.

So, for the purposes of detailed investigation of how people actually talk to one another we need to adapt and extend the standard orthography. The task is to produce transcriptions that are accurate records of all relevant features of performance.

A transcription will be effective to the extent that it can clearly and comprehensively represent those characteristics of spoken verbal interaction already identified in the previous chapter. The transcription should, then, represent those features of talk that serve to identify it as talk:

(i) produced spontaneously and without detailed conscious planning;

(ii) produced with the intention that there be some response;

(iii) designed to show for each utterance that it is either a response, is meant to elicit a response, or both;

(iv) designed to take account, on a moment-by-moment basis, of the roles of the participants, the purposes of the participants and the situation in which the talk occurs.

3.5 Making a transcription

A transcription incorporating these features can be built up in the following step-by-step fashion:

Step 1

Listen to section 25 on your *Varieties* cassette. You will hear a conversation between a vicar and a couple regarding arrangements for the couple's forthcoming marriage. Listen with the following questions in mind:

(a) Is the talk spontaneous or scripted?
(b) Is the talk produced as a monologue by just one of the speakers?
(c) Is it possible to distinguish talk that is typical of a speaker and talk that is typical of a listener?
(d) Is it possible to identify who the speakers are, what their common purposes are and what sort of place the talk is occurring in?

Discussion

Effectively you have here been overhearing someone else's conversation and a number of things will no doubt have occurred to you on listening to it for the first time. You will have noticed that most of the talking is done by one of the participants and that participant is the vicar. The participant you hear as the vicar somehow or other just sounds as you would expect a vicar to sound.

Although the vicar does most of the talking he does seem to change his role from speaker to listener/responder about halfway through before taking up the speaker role again. Even when he is in the listener/responder role, however, the vicar doesn't actually fall silent. We hear him doing things just as we hear the other two participants, Tom and Marion, doing things when they are in the listener/responder role.

However, you will also have noticed that when you do hear someone it is by no means always the case that that someone is producing recognisable words. Sometimes you hear what are probably deep in-breaths, sometimes laughter, sometimes non-word vocalisations like *er*, *erm*, *mm* and the like. Sometimes words are begun but not finished as speakers abandon or restart what they were apparently about to say. It can also happen that you 'hear' gaps or silences in the talk. Even when the speakers are producing words it's not always clear just what they are saying. This is often the case when they are talking at the same time as someone else.

With regard to making sense of what is going on you will, no doubt, have got some idea of what the participants are up to even though you are, as it were, eavesdropping part-way through someone else's conversation. I get the impression that overall the vicar has been trying to get information from the couple about their attitudes to marriage whilst at the same time impressing on them his own attitude towards it. They in their turn seem to have been concerned with impressing on him that they have attitudes similar to his own. The situation in which the talk is taking place would seem to be indoors in some such place as a quiet office or private study – on the evidence of the recording we can hear no extraneous sounds such as radios, traffic, other conversations in the background etc.

This set of observations that I have just made are, I am sure, observations that most of us would feel confident in making. The observations are, of course, based entirely on what is hearable in the talk. And what is heard shows clearly that the talk is spontaneous, that speakers produce their talk with the expectation that it will be responded to, that participants come to the talk with certain predetermined roles, that they take on and give up certain roles in the course of the talk, and that the participants are using the talk to achieve particular purposes in a particular setting. Our transcription should record all those features of the talk that lead us to hear it in this way.

Step 2

Listen to section 25 again. But this time, using the pause and review button on your cassette player, write down everything which you would count as the vicar's behavour. Write it down in the order in which it occurs. This should include the words he uses, his unfinished words, his non-word vocalisations, the in-breaths you hear him produce and the silences which you hear and which you feel are attributable to him and not one of the other speakers. Such a silence would be, for example, the sort that occurs part-way through the production of a sentence or a phrase and where it is obvious from the sense or grammar of what has been said that there is more to come.

Use the standard alphabetic orthography to represent his words and part-completed words. At the cut-off point of part-completed words you should place a '-'.

Non-word vocalisations should be represented as appropriate with *er, erm, mm, heheheh*, etc.

For any in-breaths that you hear use ˙h, increasing the number used as a way of showing the intensity with which the in-breath appears to have been produced, e.g. ˙h˙h˙h˙h. In the case of audible outbreaths use h˙ h˙.

Do not use commas, question marks, full stops, etc. To indicate a silence of less than half a second use (.). For silences of half a second or more that you can time indicate the length of silence in seconds within brackets (0.5), (1.0), (1.5), etc.

Where you cannot make out at all what has been said but you are sure that there is something then simply use empty brackets with asterisks denoting the number of syllables heard (********).

Where you hear someone else doing something then indicate who it is but at this stage leave a space rather than transcribe what they are actually doing.

Discussion

A first transcription of the vicar's talk

Vicar	I've been watching (.) you know
	the (1.0) programme on TV (1.0) I'm not
Marion	
Tom	
	preaching at you (.) but as a
	minister of the (.) church that erm (.)
Tom	
	I naturally ˙h stand for the
	Christian doctrine of marriage (1.0) and

Tom	
	erm (.) you are sincere in that you
	want to (.) marry (.) Marion (1.0) and really
Tom	
	make a go of it (.) that is so
Tom	
	isn't it
Tom	
Vicar	Yes
Tom	
Vicar	Yes (0.5) Good
Tom	
Vicar	That's right (0.5) Yes (.) You'll
	remember for many a day (.)
	for the vows that you've
	made to each other (0.5) because
	i- although it's a simple
	service it's a profound service
Tom	
Marion	

This transcription, you will notice, is set out much as the dialogue of a play would be with blocks of transcribed talk corresponding to the participants' apparently alternating turns at speaking.

You will also have noticed that unlike in ordinary written texts I have restricted the use of capital letters to the names of people, standard abbreviations, the first person singular subject pronoun *I*, and the initial letter of what I have taken to be the first word in a participant's turn at speaking. The capital has not been used to mark sentence beginnings since we are not operating with the sentence as a unit of transcription.

Examples

    Vicar   erm (.) you are sincere in that you
→ want to (.) marry (.) **Marion** (1.0) and really

Notice here the capital letter for the word *Marion*.

    → *Vicar*   the programme on *TV* (1.0) I'm not

Notice here the standard abbreviation *TV*

→ *Vicar*   the programme on TV (1.0) **I**'m not

Notice here the use of a capital for the first person subject pronoun *I*.

→ *Vicar*   **That**'s right (0.5) **Yes** (.) **You**'ll

Notice here that this one line contains three turns at speaking and capitals are used for the first words in each turn, i.e. *That, Yes* and *You*. A turn at speaking need not be a sentence.

Of course, a participant's turn can extend over several lines and over the talk of other speakers. Where I have heard what some participant is doing as a continuation of that participant's previously started turn at speaking then a capital letter has not been used at the beginning of the continuation.

Examples

→ *Vicar*   **preaching** at you (.) **but** as a

Notice here that *preaching* has no capital because despite the fact that it is written at the beginning of a new line it cannot in any way be heard as the start of a new turn. *But* is also written without a capital because despite the fact that it occurs immediately after a pause it can clearly be heard as a continuation of a turn that a participant has already started.

Vicar   Christian doctrine of marriage (1.0) and
Tom
→ *Vicar*   erm (.) **you** are sincere in that you

Notice here that *you* is not written with a capital because it has been made quite clear through his use of *and* that what he says next is intended by the vicar to be heard as a continuation of his turn. And this despite the fact that Tom can be heard to be doing something over the vicar's talk.

In addition to my restricted use of capital letters you will also have noticed that, as suggested, I have not used commas, full stops, question marks and the like. Turns at speaking, or parts of turns at speaking, are thus not treated as equivalent to the sentence units of written texts. (What we should treat as a turn at speaking will be discussed in more detail in a later chapter.)

Step 3

Listen to section 25 again. This time concentrate on the way in which words and sequences of words are actually pronounced. Specifically you should listen for:

(i) distinctive pronunciations of individual sound segments within words (consonants or vowels), e.g. the pronunciation of *the* as either *th(uh)* or *th(ee)*;

(ii) segments, syllables (*an-ti-dis-es-tab-lish-ment-ar-ian-ism*), words or word sequences that are particularly loud relative to surrounding talk;

(iii) segments, syllables, words or sequences of words that are particularly strong stress relative to surrounding talk;

(iv) segments, syllables, words or sequences of words that have particularly strong stress relative to surrounding talk;

(v) segments, syllables, words of sequences of words that have particularly raised or lowered pitch relative to surrounding talk;

(vi) syllables on which a falling, rising, or falling and rising pitch is particularly apparent;

(vii) vowels or consonants whose pronunciation is held for a particularly long time giving the impression that their distinctive sound has been 'stretched' or 'drawled'.

So long as you provide a key with your transcription explaining what you are using them to refer to you can really choose any symbols you like to indicate the above features. Some suggestions:

(i) for distinctive segmental pronunciations you can either devise your own phoneticised spellings, though in this case be aware of the difficulties illustrated earlier, or use the more standardised phonetic symbols such as those used in *Varieties of English* and other texts as a basis for making broad phonetic transcriptions of RP English. These symbols at least have the merit of having universally accepted values and can be precisely associated with particular articulatory movements and articulatory settings.

	Vowels			*Consonants*	
i	as in RP	bead	p	as in RP	**p**it
ɪ	as in RP	bid	b	as in RP	**b**it
ɛ	as in RP	bed	t	as in RP	**t**ip
aɛ	as in RP	bad	d	as in RP	**d**id
ɑː	as in RP	hard	k	as in RP	**k**ick
ɒ	as in RP	cod	g	as in RP	**g**ive
ɔ	as in RP	cau**g**ht	f	as in RP	**f**ive
ʊ	as in RP	put	v	as in RP	**v**ine
uː	as in RP	sh**oe**	θ	as in RP	**th**umb
ʌ	as in RP	cup	ð	as in RP	**th**is
ɜː	as in RP	bird	s	as in RP	**s**ome
ə	as in RP	**a**bout/	z	as in RP	**z**oo
	(the schwa)	port**er**	ʃ	as in RP	**sh**op
ɛɪ	as in RP	pay	ʒ	as in RP	mea**s**ure
aɪ	as in RP	pie	h	as in RP	**h**ot
ɔɪ	as in RP	boy	tʃ	as in RP	**ch**arge
əʊ	as in RP	go	dʒ	as in RP	**g**in
aʊ	as in RP	hound	m	as in RP	**m**ouse
iə	as in RP	beer	n	as in RP	**n**ice
ɛə	as in RP	bear	ŋ	as in RP	si**ng**
ʊə	as in RP	cure	l	as in RP	**l**eaf
			r	as in RP	**r**un
			j	as in RP	**y**acht
			w	as in RP	**w**et

For example:

→ saw /ði/ erm boy
(distinctive pronunciation of *the* before a noun beginning with a consonant)

(ii) loudness – capitalise that part of an item's standard orthographic spelling that is particularly loud, for example:

→ MUMMY I want to wee wee

(iii)   quietness – place a raised '°' before and after the quietly said item, for example:

     → MUMMY I want to °wee wee°

(iv)   stress – underline the item that receives particular stress, for example:

     → MUMMY I <u>want</u> to °wee wee°

(v)   pitch height – place ↑ for raised pitch height before and after the relevant item;
place ↓ for lowered pitch height before and after the relevant item, for example:

     → ↑MUMMY↑ I <u>want</u> to °wee wee°

(vi)   pitch movement – place ´ above the vowel of the syllable that you want to pick out as having a note that is noticeably rising; ` above the vowel of a syllable that you want to pick out as having a note that is noticeably falling; ^ for a vowel whose note first rises then falls; and ᵛ for a vowel whose note first falls then rises, for example:

     → ↑MUMMY↑ I <u>wânt</u> to °wee wee°

(vii)   stretched segments – place a colon after a segment that has been held for longer what seems normal for the speaker, adding to the number of colons to indicate extra stretching, for example:

     → ↑MUMMY::↑ I   <u>wânt</u> to °wee wee°

A revised transcription of the vicar's talk

Vicar	I've been <u>watchi</u>ng: (.) you know
	/ði/ (1.0) programme on TV (1.0) I'm <u>not</u>
Marion	
Tom	
	<u>preachi</u>ng at you (.) ↑but↑ as a
	minister of /ðiː/ (.) chur:ch that erm (.)
Tom	
	↑I↑ naturally •h <u>stand</u> for the
	Christian <u>doctri</u>ne of <u>marri</u>age (1.0) and

49

Tom	
	erm (.) you <u>are</u>:: sincere:: in that
	you want /tu:/ (.) <u>marry</u> (.) <u>M</u>arion (1.0) and really
Tom	
	make a <u>go</u> of it (.) <u>that</u> is <u>so</u>
Tom	
	isn't it
Tom	
Vicar	Yè:s
Tom	
Vicar	Yè:s (0.5) Good
Tom	
Vicar	That's right (0.5) Yè:s (.) ↑You'll↑
	re<u>mem</u>ber for many a day:: (.)
	for the <u>vows</u> that you've
	<u>made</u> to each other (0.5) because
	i- ↑al↑ though it's a <u>simple</u>
	service it's a <u>profound</u> service
Tom	
Marion	

Just as it is unlikely that two people will give identical accounts of what in their view was the essential gist of a conversation, so it is most unlikely that any two transcribers will pick on precisely the same features to represent in their transcriptions. It's unlikely that they will even notice all the same features.

What you notice will to some extent depend on the particular purposes for which the transcription is to be used. Of course, the purposes that people will bring to the task of making a transcription can in turn depend on the experience that they already have in listening to and analysing talk. In other words, no transcription can ever be a wholly innocent recording of just anything and everything that is there on the tape. We are inevitably selective.

I suppose that in picking on the particular features I have picked on in the vicar's talk I have been guided by a concern to bring out those features of talk we discussed in general terms earlier, features that indicate spontaneity, the roles of the participant, and the purposes the participant is seeking to achieve within the interactional episode.

For example, I have chosen in my transcript to indicate that the words *the* and *to* are distinctively pronounced at certain points in the vicar's talk:

→ *Vicar*   you know /ði/ (1.0) programme on TV
→ *Vicar*   ↑but↑ as a minister of /ðiː/ (.)
              chur:ch
→ *Vicar*   you are:: sincere in that you
              want /tuː/ (.) marry (.) Marion

In each case where we see words produced with distinctive vowel sounds we can see that there is an immediately following pause preceding the grammatically required next items; respectively the nouns *programme* and *church*, and the verb *marry*. The pauses at these points of grammatical incompleteness are, of course, indicators that the talk is spontaneous. The use of the full vowel forms for *the* and *to* rather than the reduced *schwa* forms /ðə/ and /tə/ are one way for the speaker to show that pauses, though indicators of spontaneity, can be planned for and their impending occurrence in the flow of talk signalled.

As another example of how I have inevitably been selective in my noting of features, consider the very little use I have made of the symbols for marking pitch movement.

→ *Vicar*   Yè:s
→ *Vicar*   Yè:s
→ *Vicar*   That's right (0.5) Yè:s

When the vicar produces the words with these pitch movements he does so when in the role of listener and more precisely when in the role of listener who is not desperately trying to get the role of speaker at this particular point in the conversation. The pitch movements marked on these words used in isolation would thus seem to have something to do with the vicar's current role in the conversation. They seem to be an indication of his acceptance of that role, i.e. the role of continuing listener.

As a final illustration of my selectivity I would like to draw your attention to my marking of stress and the stretching of segments. Stress and stretching seem to be related in some way to the vicar's purpose of preaching to the couple, and this despite what he says at the beginning. The stress placements and use of stretching give the vicar's talk that rhythmic quality so distinctive of those talking to a captive audience, be it from the pulpit, to a class of children, or a televised news report:

→	*Vicar*	↑You'll↑ remember for many a day:: (.)
→		for the <u>vows</u> that you've <u>made</u>
→		to each other (0.5) because
→		i- ↑al↑though it's a <u>simple</u> service
→		it's a pro<u>found</u> service

We must accept then that no transcription can ever be complete in the sense that every feature available to the listener will be recorded in the written form. Transcribers will differ with respect to their own experience, perceptions and purposes. The purpose that was, as it were, at the back of my mind in making the above transcription was to be in a position to illustrate with my transcription some very general features of the talk. More specific purposes would inevitably lead to concentration on more detail with regard to selected features.

For example, if the talk is between mothers and their very young children, interest might well be in how the mothers deal with 'errors' in the talk of their children. This would necessitate a very detailed transcription of any distinctively pronounced individual sound segments in the children's talk since these clearly would be crucial in the mothers' recognition that they have an error to deal with. Or, again, the interest might be in how children ask parents for things and it would be likely that children would make much use of variations in pitch in doing this and this would then need to be focused on and transcribed.

Step 4

Repeat steps 1 to 3 for the talk produced by Marion and Tom.

A first transcription incorporating Marion and Tom's talk

Vicar	I've been <u>watching</u>: (.) you know
	/ði/ (1.0) programme on TV (1.0) I'm <u>not</u>
Marion	AHUH
Tom	The programme mm
Vicar	<u>preaching</u> at you (.) ↑but↑ as a
	minister of /ðiː/ (.) chur:ch that erm (.)
Tom	mm yè:s

Vicar	↑I↑ naturally ˙h <u>stand</u> for the
	<u>Christ</u>ian <u>doct</u>rine of <u>marri</u>age (1.0) and
Tom	<u>mm</u>
Vicar	erm (.) you <u>are</u>:: sincere in that
	you want /tuː/ marry (.) Marion (1.0) and really
Tom	mmyèah
Vicar	make a <u>go</u> of it (.) <u>that</u> is <u>so</u>
Tom	Oh
Vicar	isn't it
Tom	Oh
Vicar	isn't it
Tom	↑Oh↑ <u>that</u> is so yeah we- ↑I mean↑ we
Vicar	Yè:s
Tom	<u>defin</u>itely <u>do</u> intend to: (.) ˙h <u>make</u>
	a go of it there (0.5) I mean
Vicar	Yè:s (0.5) Good
Tom	we are d- (.) ↑we've↑ been
	intending to get married for a lo- (.)
	↑quite↑ a ↑whi:le↑ now like you know
Vicar	That's right (0.5) Yè:s (.) ↑You'll↑
	re<u>mem</u>ber for many a day:: (.)
	for the <u>vows</u> that you've
	<u>made</u> to each other (0.5) because
	i- ↑al↑ though it's a <u>simple</u>
	service it's a pro<u>found</u> service
Tom	mm
Marion	mm

Discussion

You will have noticed that some of Tom's pronunciation is non-standard but I have chosen not to mark this in my transcription. Our purpose in making the transcription is to be able to focus on features that characterise the talk as typical of spontaneous spoken verbal interaction. The non-standard pronunciations seem to be a permanent feature of Tom's talk, features of his social/regional accent, and do not seem to have any special relevance in typing this talk as either spontaneous or interactional. Of course, if our aim had been to compare Tom's talk when in the presence of a vicar at a more or less formal meeting with Tom's talk in the pub when in conversation with friends then the transcription would need to have brought features of non-standard pronunciation into much sharper focus.

However, something that does have clear relevance for the conduct of the interaction is the timing of the participants' talk relative to each other's. Sometimes there is a clearly heard gap or 'beat' between one speaker's talk and the next; sometimes there is no such 'beat' and a following speaker's talk is **latched** on to the prior speaker's with not even a minutely discernible gap; and sometimes the speakers actually talk at the same time and produce what we can refer to as **overlapping** talk.

All sorts of inferences that we make when talking to someone can hinge on whether their talk clearly waits for our own talk's completion, is produced almost, but not quite, before we have finished or indeed very obviously before we have finished. Depending on how people time their talk relative to one another's we can hear people as being supportive, pushy, downright interruptive or a host of other things.

Step 5

Listen to the extract again and indicate whether a speaker's talk is latched to or overlaps with prior talk.

(i) latched talk – can be indicated by placing an '=' sign at the end of a speaker's talk and at the beginning of the following speaker's talk to which it is latched, for example:

> *Child* Can I have an ice-cream =
> *Mother* = 'Course you can

(ii) overlapping talk – can be indicated by placing square brackets round two speakers' overlapping talk, for example:

> *Vicar* programme⌈ on   T⌉V
> *Tom*   ⌊ The programme⌋

A first transcription incorporating Marion and Tom's talk

Vicar	I've been <u>watch</u>ing: (.) you know
	/ði/ ⌈ (1.0) ⌉ programme ⌈ on T ⌉V ⌈ (1.0) ⌉
	⌊ AHUH ⌋ ⌊ The programme ⌋ ⌊ mm ⌋
	I'm not
Marion	
Tom	
Vicar	<u>preach</u>ing at you (.) ↑but↑ as a
	minister of ⌈ /ði/ ⌉ (.) <u>chur:ch</u> that erm (.)
Tom	⌊ mm yè:s ⌋
Vicar	↑I↑ naturally ˙h <u>stand</u> for the
	<u>Christian</u> <u>doctrine</u> of <u>marriage</u> ⌈ (1.0) ⌉ and
Tom	⌊ mm ⌋
Vicar	erm (.) you <u>are</u>:: sincere in that
	you want /tuː/ <u>marry</u> (.) Marion ⌈ (1.0) ⌉ and really
	⌊ mmyèah ⌋
Tom	
Vicar	make a <u>go</u> of it (.) <u>that</u> is s⌈o ⌉
Tom	⌊oh⌋
Vicar	isn't it =
Tom	= ↑Oh↑ <u>that</u> is so yeah ⌈ we- ⌉ ↑I mean↑ we
Vicar	⌊ Yès ⌋
Tom	<u>definitely</u> <u>do</u> intend to: (.) ˙h <u>make</u>
	a go of it there ⌈ (0.5) ⌉ I ⌈ mean ⌉
Vicar	⌊ Yès ⌋ (0.5) ⌊ Good ⌋
Tom	we are d- (.) ↑we've↑ been
	intending to get married for a lo- (.)
	↑quite↑ a <u>whi:le</u> now like ⌈ you know ⌉
Vicar	⌊ That's right ⌋
	(0.5) Yè:s (.) ↑You'll↑
	<u>remem</u>ber for many a day:: (.)
	for the <u>vows</u> that you've
	<u>made</u> to each other (0.5) because
	i- ↑al↑though it's a <u>simple</u>
	service it's a pro<u>found</u> service =
Tom	= mm =
Marion	= mm

In making this transcription we have done what most investigators do when making their initial transcriptions of interactional episodes. That is, we have produced a transcription that is comprehensive in the sense that it records the range of features that are to be heard in any stretch of spontaneous talk. So the transcription has noted certain distinctive segmental pronunciations, in-breaths you can sometimes hear, stressed or stretched sounds, differing pitch levels and movements in pitch level, loud speech and soft speech, and talk produced in overlap. Comprehensive but not completely detailed transcriptions such as the one we have produced can then be refined as particular phenomena in the talk are focused on.

Activity 3.9

Compare the following transcript of the conversational extract from *Heartburn* with the transcript of the vicar, Tom and Marion and show with reference to the transcribed details how one is an example of spontaneous talk whilst the other is an example of scripted talk.

Heartburn – a transcription

Betty   I found ou::t ˙h <u>who</u> Thelma Rice is having the affair
        with
        (1.0)

Rachel   ↑An::↑ could I have a pound of your ↑<u>sausage</u>↑ too
        ↑please↑
        (1.0)
        ↓Òh↓
        (0.5)

Betty   You're ↑not↑ go::nna ↑like↑ it
        (0.5)

Rachel   ↑Who is it↑

Betty   ↑Ar↑ thur
        (1.0)

Rachel   Arthur Siegel
        (0.5)

Betty   They were <u>seen</u> having ↑<u>drinks</u>↑ at the Washington
        <u>Hil</u>ton the other day now <u>nobody</u> has drinks at the
        <u>Washington</u> <u>Hil</u>ton <u>unless</u> <u>something</u> ↑<u>sec</u>↑ ret's going
        o::n

Rachel	•h•h•h (clears throat) <u>Arthur</u> is not having an affair with ↓Thelma Rice↓
Betty	↑How do you know this↓
Rachel	I <u>just</u> know
	(5.0)
Betty	↑Tell me::↑ =
Rachel	= ↑OK↑ but you got to <u>prom</u>ise me you won't tell anyone
Betty	I •h•h promise
	(2.0)
Rachel	h•h•h• I saw <u>Thelma</u> at the gynecologist's:: she has a h:::orrible in<u>fec</u>tion (.) do you wanna know about it
	(0.5)
Betty	↑Wh-↑ (.) ↑Oh Go:::d↑
	(0.5)
Rachel	She made me <u>prom</u>ise not to <u>tell</u> anybody
	(0.5)
	↑She al::↑ most didn't have to because it was so:: dis<u>gust</u>ing I almost ⌈ couldn't
Child	⌊ ↑Mummy:::↑ ⌉↑huh↑ (.) ↑huh↑ (.) ↑huh↑
Rachel	I'm only telling you ↑because↑ (.) I <u>want</u> you to know it's not <u>true</u> about <u>her</u> and <u>Arthur</u>
	(0.5)
Betty	Well then w- ↑why↑ was she having (.) ↑a drink↑ with him::
	(0.5)
Rachel	↑↑She probably↑↑ ↑wanted some legal↑ ad<u>vice</u> h•h•
	(1.0)
	Y- y'know be ↑cause she got↑ /ði/ er (.) infection in a restaurant h•h•
	(0.5)
	a ↑Viet↑ namese restaurant
Betty	Not the ↑one↑ on <u>Kay</u> street
	(0.5)
Rachel	S- ↑<u>some</u>↑ where in Virginia and <u>she</u> ↑wants↑ to sue them
	(1.5)

Betty	She get it from the ↑toi↑ let seat or from something ↑she↑ ate or °what° (0.5)
Rachel	From the <u>toi</u>let seat I ⌈ guess
Betty	⌊ Ah::::::⌋::
Rachel	Oh well I'm not <u>sure</u>::
	(0.5)
	Maybe from the <u>spring</u> rolls
	(0.5)
Betty	Oh God
Child	(****)
Rachel	↑↑Ye::s↑↑ (.) oh ↑<u>huhu</u>hu↑
	(0.5)
Betty	I feel <u>so</u>:: sorry for her
Rachel	↑Don't↑ feel (.) <u>too</u> sorry for:: ↑her↑ (.) it's curable
	(0.5)
	<u>E</u>ventually

4. Seeing the organisation of talk

4.1 Introduction

A transcription such as the one developed in the previous chapter is a 'freeze-frame' of talk as it occurs in spoken verbal interaction. It enables us to observe and compare simultaneously a variety of phenomena in the talk.

We could, for example, look at the apparent non-fluency features such as hesitations, pauses, false starts, recycling of material etc., and investigate how and why they come to be incorporated into talk that is spontaneously produced. We could look at how speakers bring it about that they usually, though not always, talk when the other participants are silent. We could look at how speakers indicate to others that they are content to listen, that they want to say something, and what it is that they want to say. Phenomena related to these and other issues will be investigated in detail in later chapters.

For the moment, the use to which a transcription such as the one we have produced can be put can be demonstrated by investigating just one particular phenomenon. I have already suggested that a transcription can be used to confirm a hypothesis, i.e. to provide evidence to confirm that what we think might happen really does in practice. But transcriptions can also be used to refine a hypothesis, or indeed, to provide a basis for formulating a hypothesis in the first place. It is this third possibility that I now want to explore.

4.2 Raised voices

At several points in the talk it can be seen from the transcription that a particular phenomenon recurs. Individual words or parts of words are produced with raised pitch. I want to investigate why some parts of the talk might be produced in this way. Is it because the speaker is angry? Is it because the speaker wants what he or she is saying to be treated as a question? Is it because the speaker wants to show surprise? Or is it something quite different from these possibilities? Close inspection of our transcription should be able to throw some light on the matter.

We can begin by listing those fragments of the talk we have transcribed where the phenomenon we want to investigate occurs.

Fragment 1

→ *Vicar*   preaching at you (.) ↑but↑ as a

 Tom   minister of [/ðiː/] (.) chur:ch that erm (.)
            [mm yèːs]

→ *Vicar*   ↑I↑ naturally ˙h stand for the
            Christian doctrine of marriage

Fragment 2

 Vicar   [(1.0)   ] and really
 Tom   [mmyèah]

 Vicar   make a go of it (.) that is s[o]
 Tom   [Oh]

 Vicar   isn't it =

→ *Tom*   = ↑Oh↑ that is so yeah [we-] ↑I mean↑ we
 Vicar   [Yès]

 Tom   definitely do intend to: (.) h̆ make

           a go of it there [(0.5)]   I [mean]
 Vicar   [Yèːs] (0.5)   [Good]

→ *Tom*   we are d- (.) ↑we've↑ been
           intending to get married for a lo- (.)

→   ↑quite↑ a whi:le now like you know

Fragment 3

→ *Tom*   ⎡ You know ⎤
                 ⎣ That's right ⎦

Vicar

→   (0.5) Yè:s (.) ↑you'll↑
         remember for many a day:: (.)
         for the <u>vows</u> that you've
         <u>made</u> to each other (0.5) because
         i- ↑al↑though it's a <u>simple</u>
         service it's a pro<u>found</u> service =

4.3 Locating instances of a phenomenon

An obvious first step to take is to establish precisely where each item with raised pitch occurs. We can do this by detailing what immediately precedes and what immediately follows the items which are pronounced with the raised pitch.

Activity 4.1 _____

Consider the first fragment in which the items with particularly raised pitch occur and describe precisely the places within the talk that they occur:

Fragment 1

Vicar   (1.0) I'm not
→   <u>preaching</u> at you (.) ↑but↑ as a
         minister of ⎡ /ðiː/   ⎤ (.) chur:ch that erm (.)
Tom   ⎣ mm yès ⎦
→ *Vicar*   Vicar ↑I↑ naturally ˙h <u>stand</u> for the
         <u>Christ</u>ian <u>doct</u>rine of <u>marri</u>age

Discussion

We can make the following observations. The item ↑*but*↑ occurs immediately after a micropause and at the very beginning, or what we might refer to as the **clause initial position**, of what is a new clause structure.

We can also note that the talk immediately preceding the item ↑*but*↑ is itself preceded by a one-second pause and is produced as a sort of aside or **parenthetical** comment to the main thrust of what the vicar is saying. *I'm not preaching at you* is in effect a comment by the vicar on how he wants what he is saying to be understood.

Thus we can see that the ↑*but*↑ is produced at just that point in the talk where the speaker is coming back to a line of talk already begun but temporarily abandoned at the point of the one-second pause. The ↑*but*↑ might then best be regarded as a sort of restart, resumption or continuation of an already initiated aspect of the speaker's talk.

Let's now consider the item ↑*It*↑. This occurs immediately following a micropause which itself immediately follows the non-word vocalisation *erm*. And again ↑*It*↑, the item with raised pitch, occurs in the clause initial position of a new clause.

We should also note that the preceding micropause and non-word vocalisation occur just as the vicar starts out to say one thing but then abandons it. How do we know this from what is said?

→ chur:ch that erm (.)

Possible grammatical completions of this might have been:

church **that believes in marriage**
church **that believes in the family**
church **that welcomes commitment for life**

In each case the grammatical completion would involve the use of a clause begun with the word *that* which relates back to and gives more information about the noun *church*. Clauses of this kind are called **relative clauses**. The following are also examples of relative clauses:

the church **which has a crooked spire**
the man **who has a crooked nose**
the church **which I saw yesterday**
the man **whom I married last week**
the church **I saw yesterday**
the man **I saw yesterday**

We can see from this that the words *that*, *which* and *who* provide a very strong signal that what is coming up is a relative clause. So, because *church* is immediately followed by *that*, this gives us good evidence that the vicar was about to say a particular sort of thing but then abandons it. The vicar was about to use a relative clause in order to modify the noun *church*.

The non-word vocalisation and micropause may thus be seen as a way of displaying to the other participants that the direction which they might expect the speaker to be taking, the speaker's **projected talk**, is under active review and may be imminently modified or even abandoned.

What we actually get is the abandonment of the projected relative clause and the initiation of a new clause. This new clause is actually so constructed that it can be heard as following directly as a coherent continuation of the talk after the word *church*.

> as a minister of the church **(that)** I naturally stand for the Christian doctrine of marriage

In other words it seems that the clause begun by the raised pitch item ↑*I*↑ is produced so as to be heard as if the item *that* introducing the projected relative clause had never occurred. The clause begun with the raised pitch ↑*I*↑ thus amounts to a restart of the talk on a line of talk already begun.

Both ↑*but*↑ and ↑*I*↑ therefore occur at places in the talk that can be described as some sort of restart. And we can justify our description of these places in the talk as in some sense involving restarts because of what immediately precedes and follows these places in the talk.

4.4 Sequential environments and interactional significance

In specifying what immediately precedes or follows something in the flow of talk we are specifying its **sequential environment**. We therefore have found raised pitch ↑*but*↑ and raised pitch ↑*I*↑ to occur in similar sequential environments. Furthermore, the specification of the relevant sequential environment tells us something about the significance which the use of raised pitch on these items might have for the participants in the interaction. Here raised pitch seems to be systematically associated with the first item to occur in a stretch of talk that is a restart.

No doubt raised pitch can be used for a variety of purposes but an initial hypothesis might be that raised pitch can be used by the speaker to indicate to his/her interactional partner that what is now about to be said is in fact a resumption of something already started. On this hypothesis one possible **interactional significance** of raised pitch is to signal restarts in spoken verbal interaction.

We should now consider more data to see if the hypothesis can be confirmed:

Activity 4.2

Describe the sequential environments and interactional significance of raised pitch in the following fragment:

Fragment 2

```
        Vicar   [ (1.0)       ] and really
        Tom     ⌊ mm yèah     ⌋

        Vicar   make a go of it (.) that is  s[ o  ]
        Tom                                   ⌊ Oh ⌋

        Vicar   isn't it =
   →    Tom     =↑Oh↑  that is so yeah [we-] ↑I mean↑ we
        Vicar                          ⌊Yès⌋

        Tom     definitely do intend to: (.) ˙h make
                a go of it there [ (0.5) ]        I [ mean  ]
        Vicar                    ⌊ Yès   ⌋ (0.5)    ⌊ Good  ⌋

   →    Tom     we are d- (.) ↑we've↑ been
                intending to get married for a lo- (.)
   →            ↑quite↑ a whi:le now like you know
```

Discussion

Tom's raised pitch item ↑*Oh*↑ occurs at the very beginning of the first clause of a new speaking turn and we can say that it is to be found in **turn initial position**. As such it immediately follows the prior speaker's talk. However, we should note that just before the vicar finished his turn Tom had tried to initiate a responding turn with *Oh*. However, this attempted response turned out to be initiated in overlap with part of the vicar's *so*:

<pre>
      Vicar   make a go of it (.) that is s⌈ o ⌉
  →   Tom   ⌊ Oh ⌋
      Vicar   isn't it =
</pre>

So in effect Tom's second Oh, the one produced with raised pitch as ↑*Oh*↑ is a restart of the turn begun but abandoned at the point where the vicar was nearing the end of his turn. Our observation of Tom's use of raised pitch on the item ↑*Oh*↑ would thus seem to confirm our hypothesis about its possible interactional significance.

The next three items with raised pitch in this fragment can be treated as a group. They all occur immediately following a word that has been cut off and each occurs in the initial position of what turns out to be a clause or phrase that can be regarded as complete in itself, i.e. as what we might call a complete **syntactic unit**:

→ yeah we- ↑I mean↑ we definitely do intend to:
→ we are d- (.) ↑we've↑ been intending to get married
→ for a lo- (.) ↑quite↑ a whi:le

Here the talk that has been projected has been cut off part-way through the pronunciation of a word and the raised pitch items would seem to signal that what comes next is an alternative to the talk as originally projected. Again the talk initiated by the raised pitch item is a sort of restart.

The third fragment contains the two sorts of restart already encountered and again the restarts are associated with raised pitch.

Activity 4.3 ————————————————————

Compare the use of raised pitch in the following fragment with its use in fragments 1 and 2:

Fragment 3

<pre>
      Tom   ⌈ You know   ⌉
      Vicar ⌊ That's right⌋
  →   (0.5) Yè:s (.) ↑you'll↑
              remember for many a day:: (.)
</pre>

for the <u>vows</u> that you've
<u>made</u> to each other (0.5) because
→   i- ↑al↑though it's a <u>simple</u>
service it's a pro<u>found</u> service=

Discussion

Here the raised pitch item ↑*you'll*↑ occurs in the initial position
of a new clause and immediately following a micropause. The
micropause itself occurs immediately following the item *Yè:s* said
with a falling pitch movement thus indicating acceptance of the
listener role. The item *Yè:s* has in turn followed a pause which
comes immediately after talk that turned out to have been said in
overlap with Tom's talk.

It seems that what is happening here is this. Tom has the
speaker role and the vicar has the role of listener. In fulfilling
this role the vicar must respond at appropriate points in ways
which allow Tom to continue in the speaker's role. This the vicar
does with his *That's right*. However, he mistimes the saying of
this somewhat and ends up saying it in overlap with Tom's *You
know*.

Since the vicar begins to speak in overlap with him Tom might
think that the vicar at this point wants to take on the speaker's
role. But the vicar has simply been responding in a minimal way
with single words, short phrases and the like, making the way
clear for Tom to continue in that role. *That's right* turns out to
be just such a minimal response.

So both Tom and the vicar have at this point in the talk a
reason for not saying anything, i.e. they assume the other has
something to say and so wants the speaking role. There thus
follows a half-second pause in which neither Tom nor the vicar
initiates any talk.

The silence is broken with the vicar's *Yè:s* which is appropriate
to his assumed role of listener and thereby offers Tom the
opportunity to continue in the role of speaker. In this role Tom
could pursue the line already projected in his talk so far. Again
no talk is initiated by Tom so the vicar restarts the conversation,
albeit in a slightly modified direction. This restart of the conver-

sation is accomplished through the use of the raised pitch ↑*You'll*↑.

The raised pitch item ↑al↑though is yet a further example of the use of raised pitch to signal a restart following a cut-off:

→ because i- ↑al↑though it's a simple service

Thus the subordinate clause projected by the use of *because*

because it's a profound service

is abandoned, restarted and becomes:

because, although it's a simple service, it's a profound service.

We have seen then that there is a pattern to the use of raised pitch in the conversation under investigation. It seems that raised pitch on an item can be used systematically by a speaker to display that talk is being restarted following some sort of break with what has gone before. Listeners should treat what follows the raised pitch item as either an alternative to or continuation of the prior material.

Now all this, of course, is only a hypothesis and will need to be checked against the evidence of other transcriptions. But the important point for us is that the hypothesis could be formulated in the first place only because the phenomenon of raised pitch and the details of its placement became apparent from inspection of our transcription.

4.5 The sequential environments and interactional significance of pauses

As a final activity in this chapter I would like you to investigate for yourself a phenomenon that occurs over and over again in this and any other transcription you will ever make. I would like you to consider the pauses in the talk of the several participants. As a guide I suggest some questions that you might approach the transcription with.

Activity 4.4

Which pauses do you think are:

(i) used to indicate grammatical structure, i.e. to punctuate the talk;

(ii) used to allow a speaker thinking-time for word search, for the planning of structure, or for the planning of content;

(iii) used for special effect such as making talk sound more rhythmical in the way it is delivered, to provide extra emphasis etc.;

(iv) used to indicate that the speaker wants something he/she has just said to be treated as an error which is to be ignored;

(v) used for any other apparent purpose.

Given the categorisation of pauses which the above questions imply:

(i) which category of pause most often occurs following a word containing a sound that is stretched?

(ii) which category of pause most often occurs at a point of overlap with another speaker's talk?

Discussion

Examples of the various categories are:

→ I'm not <u>preaching</u> at you(.) – grammatical-clause completion

→ as a minister of /ðiː/ (.) – word search

→ I mean we are d- (.) – prior talk to be treated as an error

Examples of pauses following sound stretches and pauses in overlap are:

→ I've been watching: (.) – precedes word search

→ ↑I↑ naturally •h <u>stand</u> for the <u>Christian</u> <u>doctrine</u> of <u>marri</u>age (1.0) – follows clause completion point

5. Taking turns in two-party talk

5.1 Introduction

In analysing spoken verbal interaction our central concern is the investigation of one particular sort of language use selected from the vast range of uses that we have seen the ordinary language user must be prepared for in the conduct of their daily lives. It is that sort of language use which, for most of us, figures most prominently in our daily lives.

Earlier I informally characterised this form of language use as the sort that involves people as both consumers and producers. The language produced is for the most part not subject to conscious detailed planning and is produced for instantaneous processing by some other party. It is language produced with the intention that the individual who encounters it respond in some particular sort of way. The response will in turn be produced in similar ways. And this response will be shaped on a moment-by-moment basis by the roles the individuals have or take on, by the purposes they have, and by the situation in which the talk occurs.

The essential feature of this sort of language use is that it involves at least two people doing the same sorts of things within their alternating roles of speaker and listener. It therefore differs in a very crucial respect from other uses of language, e.g. reading a book, writing a letter, speaking on the radio, watching television etc. With these uses of language one is either the producer of the language or the consumer of it, but not both. Language use in spoken verbal interaction involves two or more participants each taking on at different times, along with any other roles they may have, the **reciprocal roles** of sender of messages, the **speaker role**, and receiver of messages, the **recipient role**.

The most fundamental skill in spoken verbal interaction is the ability to step into and out of these two crucial roles as and when required. This chapter will look in detail at this vital aspect of verbal interaction – the exchange at appropriate points in interaction of the speaker and recipient roles. We shall need to show what people are doing when they are in the role of speaker; what people are doing when they are in the role of recipient; and what speakers and recipients do as they move in and out of these roles.

5.2 The turn-taking problem

The transcription we have already made looked to some extent like the script for a play. In particular, blocks of transcribed talk were set out as a succession of alternating speaker turns. However, there is a very crucial difference between the script of a play and the transcription of talk such as the one we have made. In a play it is the playwright who decides, in advance of any group of actors actually uttering anything, who shall speak, for how long, and what each speaker shall say. In the case of naturally occurring talk all this must be worked out by the participants themselves. The participants cannot know in advance who is to speak, for how long they will speak and what will be said. So any transcription of naturally occuring talk is in a sense a record of participants' solutions to these problems.

It might seem that these issues simply are not experienced as problems by participants in interaction. It's true we all know people who don't seem prepared to let anyone else get a word in edgeways, who constantly interrupt, or who seem not to pay any attention to what is being said to them. However, for the most part things seem to run smoothly and without any apparent hitch. And it is the achievement of this apparent smoothness that makes everyday verbal interaction the extraordinary achievement it is.

5.3   Dancing hands and careful gazes

The problematic nature of the exchange of speaker and recipient roles in interaction – what we might refer to as **turn-taking** – can be effectively demonstrated by considering a somewhat unusual sort of interaction. When deaf people communicate with one another over distances using teleprinters, much as hearing people do using telephones, problems of a particular kind arise with regard to turn-taking.

People who are profoundly deaf generally use some form of signing system in face-to-face interaction. Signing systems usually consist of a mixture of gestures that stand for concepts, e.g. 'man', 'run', 'happy' etc., and gestures that stand for the letters of standard orthography to make possible the spelling of names and more abstract or obscure concepts. During interaction the users of the signing system will have to take turns in signalling their messages and a range of signals – hand movements, gaze behaviour, facial expression, body posture – will be used to indicate where a transfer of turn is appropriate.

Indeed these sorts of signals undoubtedly have a role to play in the verbal interactions of hearing people.

Activity 5.1 ──────────────────────

Observe people who are holding a conversation and note down what sort of non-verbal behaviours they engage in. Decide what possible significance, if any, these behaviours might have. The best way of observing these behaviours is with the use of slow-motion playback of a video-recording.

Discussion

If you observe people talking to one another you are likely to find that the people who are talking tend to be moving their hands as they are talking but return them to 'rest' position as they are about to stop talking.

The hand movements might be being used to indicate what is being referred to – the **referents** of 'pointing' words (**deictic** terms) – like *this*, *that*, *here*, *there* etc.

Gestures can often be used as a means of representing an idea, e.g. the roundness of something, the fact that something is high, the fact that someone is mad. In order to achieve this, speakers choose gestures that either mimic the idea in question or gestures which by convention stand for the idea in question. A gesture of the first sort, or an **iconic gesture** as such gestures are sometimes referred to, would be the drawing apart of the hands of the angler wishing to describe the size of the fish he had just caught. A gesture of the second sort would be the shake of the head, conventionally associated with a denial or refusal.

Or they might be used in coordination with, and so to give extra emphasis to, key words or longer expressions that the speaker wants the recipient to take particular note of.

Finally, the movements might simply be produced as an unfocused accompaniment of the talk, simply a feature of a person's general state of animation when in the speaker role.

But however the movements are produced, it would be considered deviant for a person to produce similar movements when in the recipient role. The cessation of these movements can thus be treated by a recipient as a signal that the speaker is about to give up, or indeed has given up, the speaker role.

As for the recipient, it often happens that, when a recipient wants to indicate that he/she wishes to take on the speaker role in the course of some speaker's turn, he/she will raise a hand or tilt the head in a particular way in order to signal that the speaker should give up or 'yield' the speaking turn now (a **turn-suppressing cue**), or to indicate availability and desire for the speaking turn now (a **turn-claiming cue**).

Similarly, if you observe where people are looking (their **gaze behaviour**), during the course of verbal interaction, you will find that certain patterns emerge. You should, for example, find that recipients on the whole look towards the speaker's face during that speaker's talk, whilst the speaker's gaze will, after the initial phase of the turn, be directed elsewhere until their turn is nearly complete, at which point the speaker's gaze will be redirected to the face of the recipient so that eye contact is established.

People can initiate turns or entire conversations by taking hold of someone's arm, by leaning forward or some other major bodily movement. Turns and conversations can be brought to a close by leaning back, turning away or starting up some other activity.

However, whilst gestural behaviour would seem to be an *essential* feature of turn-taking in the face-to-face interactions of the profoundly deaf, this seems not to be the case for those with normal hearing. We can hold successful conversations with apparently smooth changes of speaker whilst otherwise occupied with our hands, e.g. in some joint task such as washing and drying dishes. More obviously, people spend vast amounts of time in our own and other modern, industrialised societies holding conversations over the telephone. Such conversations, although verbal interactions, are nevertheless not face-to-face interactions and so are interactions in which gestural behaviour can have no part to play in the management of turn-taking. There must, therefore, be some other basis than a visible gestural behaviour for the successful transfer of speaking turns in verbal interaction.

5.4 Teleprinters, turn-taking and the deaf

Profoundly deaf people can hold telephone conversations too – at least in the USA they can. Of course, the conversations are not conducted using the **auditory** (hearing) and **vocal** (voice) channels. Rather, something similar to a teleprinter system is used. Using this system the speaker will type whilst holding the speaking turn. The recipient will simultaneously read the turn as it is printed out on to paper on his/her 'receiver'. When the recipient takes on the speaker role he/she does so simply by beginning to type on to the same paper as that on which the prior speaker's message has been received.

But how does the recipient know when it is appropriate to start typing? When a full-stop appears? When the typing head stops being activated and the carriage of the typewriter moves along without printing, creating a space or gap on the paper?

Let's consider a facsimile of the typescript of the words of a conversation actually produced in this way. The conversation is between a hearing woman and her deaf daughter-in-law, Niki.

HELLO HI MOM HERE HOW IS NIKI TODAY
IM FINE   MY ARM IS SORE YES THE DOCTOR SAID
IT WOULD BE HOW IS YOUR TUMMY   I THINK IT IS

FINE   ARE YOU STILL IN PAIN NO I DONT HAVE
PAIN THAT IS GOOD TELL IAN TO BRING OVER
THAT BILL YOU GOT FROM THE BANK
AND AN OLD ONE SO I CAN SEE HOW MUCH DIF-
FERENCE YOU HAVE TO PAY MORE I HAVE TO
KNOW HOW MUCH MORE YOU ARE GOING TO
HAVE TO PAY THEM SO I KNOW WHAT IM TALK-
ING ABOUT WHEN I CALL THEM YES MY MUM
JUST TOLD ME THAT U WANTED HIM TO BRING
THE BILL ILL TELL HIM WE HAD XX HAVE TO
PAY 16$ MORE OK I WILL CALL AND FIND OUT
MORE THEY TOLD YOU IT WOULD GO UP A FEW
DOLLARS RIGHT YES BUT THEY GAVE US MORE   I
KNOW I WILL CALL AND SEE WHAT THEY CAN DO
WAIT TO SEE WHAT HAPPENS ANYWAY OK   WHEN
I DRINK TEA AND IT TASTE FUNNY IN MY TUMMY
I THINK I HAVE BLEED IN MY THROAT OH WELL
THE DOCTOR SAID IT WOULD FEEL FUNNY

OK   THAT IS ALL I HAVE TO SAY   OK TELL IAN TO
BRING THE STUFF OVER FOR ME DAD AND I WILL
BE DOWN LATER TO SEE YOU IF YOU WANT US TO
BRING A X SOMETHING FOR SUPPER TELL IAN
WHAT YOU WANT AND I WILL BRING IT OK
I THINK I WILL EAT CHICKEN NOODLE SOUP DO
YOU HAVE ENOUGH YES I HAVE ONE CAN OK
FINE WE WILL SEE YOU LATER\OK WILL SEE U
LATER BYE

Now let's imagine you are the caller, i.e. the mother-in-law, and
have dialled the number. A connection is made, your printer is
activated and prints the word *HELLO*. Your problem is to figure
out when to start typing. When you have started typing, your
daughter-in-law's problem is to figure out when she should start
typing.

Activity 5.2

Identify who says what in this typed conversation. This will give you
some idea of the problem of recognising when a speaker's turn ends.

Discussion

You probably found that at certain points it was relatively straightforward to establish who was saying what. Example 1 might be:

Niki	HELLO
Mother-in-law	HI MOM HERE HOW IS NIKI TODAY
Niki	IM FINE

At other points you may have felt sure that sequences of words represented different speaking turns without being at all sure as to whose they were. Example 2 might be:

? HOW IS YOUR TUMMY
? I THINK IT IS FINE

And at still other points you may have felt unsure as to whether a sequence of words belonged to the turn of just one speaker, or actually should have one part of the sequence allocated to one speaker and the remainder to the other. In the third example, should it be:

? YES THE DOCTOR SAID IT WOULD BE HOW IS YOUR TUMMY

or:

? YES THE DOCTOR SAID IT WOULD BE
? HOW IS YOUR TUMMY

In the case of example 1 the problem of specifying who is saying what is relatively straightforward, because we know that Niki is the person who has been called and is in the position of needing to 'open the channel' and no more.

Niki	HELLO
Mother-in-law	HI MOM HERE HOW IS NIKI TODAY
Niki	IM FINE

The single word *HELLO* can do this for her. She could, but need not, go on to identify herself.

The mother-in-law must then in some way identify herself as the caller. We should note too that if persons who have been called do not identify themselves as they 'open the channel', then the caller can try to elicit an identification. This they can do either explicitly by asking a question, e.g. *Who am I speaking to?*, or implicitly by saying something that embodies an assumption or, as we might say, **presupposes** that the person the caller intended to answer the call, i.e. the called, actually is the person who has answered.

We can thus recognise three things going on here, three things that we would expect to find people doing at this point in a telephone conversation in the following sequence of words:

HI
MOM HERE
HOW IS NIKI TODAY

We have a return of the **greeting** that opened the channel expressed in the single word *HI*; we have **self-identification** of the caller expressed in the phrase *MOM HERE*; and we have **identification of the called** expressed in the sentence *HOW IS NIKI TODAY*.

Example 2 is slightly different:

? HOW IS YOUR TUMMY
? I THINK IT IS FINE

The words of the conversation provide some, but not very strong, evidence as to who is speaking. We might, for example, expect that as a rule people making a call will seek an up-date on the called person's health somewhere towards the beginning of a call. But this only *may* happen, and is in no way a requirement.

Nevertheless we can be fairly sure that two different speakers' turns are involved here. And again it's a matter of what is being done with the words. In this case it is fairly clear that one speaker is seeking an up-date on the other speaker's state of health, and is doing this by asking a specific question. The other speaker provides the up-date by answering the question. Of course, the syntax, i.e. the use of **interrogative** sentence structure, helps us to determine that a specific question is being asked here.

The problem with example 3 arises because we recognise that speakers might want to be doing more than just one thing at a particular point in a conversation.

? YES THE DOCTOR SAID IT WOULD BE HOW IS YOUR TUMMY

or:

? YES THE DOCTOR SAID IT WOULD BE
? HOW IS YOUR TUMMY

There could either be just one speaker involved here or there could be two. If there is just one speaker then in what she is saying she must be carrying out two activities. One of the activities is accomplished through the use of:

YES THE DOCTOR SAID IT WOULD BE

whilst the other is accomplished through the use of:

HOW IS YOUR TUMMY

A speaker can combine activities in two ways. On completion of one activity the speaker can simply carry on within the same turn to carry out an additional but independent activity. Or the speaker can break some activity down into component parts that are interdependent. One example of interdependent components within the following speaking turn might be:

A   TELL IAN TO BRING OVER THAT BILL YOU GOT FROM THE BANK AND AN OLD ONE SO I CAN SEE HOW MUCH DIFFERENCE YOU HAVE TO PAY MORE
B   I HAVE TO KNOW HOW MUCH MORE YOU ARE GOING TO HAVE TO PAY THEM SO I KNOW WHAT IM TALKING ABOUT WHEN I CALL THEM

Here it seems that in the component designated A, the speaker is making a request, whilst in B the speaker is justifying the making of the request.

Now if example 3 is construed as involving just one speaking turn, then it must involve two distinct activities rather than interdependent components. The speaker might, for example, be using the one speaking turn both to acknowledge what has just been said in an immediately prior turn, and to make a further enquiry. Neither part depends on the other for its production.

Acknowledgement: YES THE DOCTOR SAID IT WOULD BE

Enquiry: HOW IS YOUR TUMMY

The problem of recognising when a speaking turn is complete is really, then, the problem of:

(i) recognising what it is that a speaker is trying to do at a particular point in a conversation;

(ii) recognising the precise point at which what the speaker is trying to do has actually been done, e.g. through the completion of single words, phrases, sentences or combinations of these.

It should be clear from this discussion that any speaking turn can be extended indefinitely beyond any given point at which a recipient could reasonably decide that what the speaker was trying to do was now complete. This can happen in three ways.

Firstly, a speaker can always add to the linguistic material used to perform an activity, even after the point where that activity is recognisably complete. An example of this from the conversation under investigation would be:

IF YOU WANT US TO BRING A X SOMETHING FOR SUPPER TELL IAN WHAT YOU WANT + AND I WILL BRING IT OK

I have placed a '+' symbol at the place where it would be reasonable to suppose that the speaker has completed what she is trying to do with the speaking turn, i.e. here the speaker would seem to be trying to offer to do something. But as this place is passed, the speaker adds more material which does not modify what she is doing in any way. She is still doing no more than making an offer.

Secondly, a speaker can extend a turn by the addition of a dependent component part or parts. An example would be the one mentioned earlier:

TELL IAN TO BRING OVER THAT BILL YOU GOT FROM THE BANK
AND AN OLD ONE SO I CAN SEE HOW MUCH DIFFERENCE YOU HAVE TO PAY MORE + I HAVE TO
KNOW HOW MUCH MORE YOU ARE GOING TO HAVE TO

PAY THEM SO I KNOW WHAT IM TALKING ABOUT
WHEN
I CALL THEM

Again the '+' symbol marks one of the places where the turn could reasonably have been supposed to be complete. The material added at this point constitutes the doing of a distinctive, though related, activity with regard to what was being done earlier in the turn.

Thirdly, a speaker can extend a turn by combining two or more independent activities. An example would be the previously discussed

HI + MOM HERE + HOW IS NIKI TODAY

These activities which speakers combine to form their speaking turns have been called **turn constructional units** – the units out of which turns at speaking are constructed. The problem for the recipient then is to know just when this process of extension by the addition of turn constructional units is or is not to be used by the speaker. We can hypothesise that to extend a turn is an option always open to the speaker, and that because this is the case it really must be for the speaker to indicate when the option will not be exercised. We can call the point at which an activity being done by a speaker is recognisably complete a place where there may, but need not be, a **transition** from one speaker to another, i.e. a *possible* **turn transition place**.

Our hypothesis, then, is that there will be some means under the control of the speaker for converting possible turn transition places into places where a turn transition actually occurs.

Let's look again at the typewritten conversation. When I presented it before I said it was a facsimile of the typescript of the words used. In fact I purposely omitted certain other non-word items which will now be included.

HELLO HI GA MOM HERE HOW IS NIKI TODAY GA
IM FINE MY ARM IS SORE GA YES THE DOCTOR
SAID IT WOULD BE HOW IS YOUR TUMMY GA I
THINK IT IS FINE GA   ARE YOU STILL IN PAIN GA
NO I DONT HAVE PAIN GA THAT IS GOOD TELL
IAN TO BRING OVER THAT BILL YOU GOT FROM
THE BANK AND AN OLD ONE SO I CAN SEE HOW

MUCH DIFFERENCE YOU HAVE TO PAY MORE I
HAVE TO KNOW HOW MUCH MORE YOU ARE
GOING TO HAVE TO PAY THEM SO I KNOW WHAT
IM TALKING ABOUT WHEN I CALL THEM GA YES
MY MUM JUST TOLD ME THAT U WANTED HIM TO
BRING THE BILL ILL TELL HIM   WE HAD XX HAVE
TO PAY 16$ MORE GA OK I WILL CALL AND FIND
OUT MORE THEY TOLD YOU IT WOULD GO UP A
FEW DOLLARS RIGHT GA YES BUT THEY GAVE US
MORE GA I KNOW I WILL CALL AND SEE WHAT
THEY CAN DO WAIT TO SEE WHAT HAPPENS ANY-
WAY GA OK WHEN I DRINK TEA AND IT TASTE
FUNNY IN MY TUMMY I THINK I HAVE BLEED IN
MY THROAT GA OH WELL THE DOCTOR SAID IT
WOULD FEEL FUNNY

OK   THAT IS ALL I HAVE TO SAY GA OK TELL IAN
TO BRING THE STUFF OVER FOR ME DAD AND I
WILL BE DOWN LATER TO SEE YOU IF YOU WANT
US TO BRING A X SOMETHING FOR SUPPER TELL
IAN WHAT YOU WANT AND I WILL BRING IT OK
GA
I THINK I WILL EAT CHICKEN NOODLE SOUP GA
DO YOU HAVE ENOUGH GA YES I HAVE ONE CAN
GA OK FINE WE WILL SEE YOU LATER GA OR SK
OK WILL SEE U LATER BYE GA TO SKSKSKSKSK

You will notice that the letters GA occur throughout the typescript. However, they do not occur randomly. Rather they occur only at possible turn transition places. And it turns out that when they do occur, there is a transition from one speaker to another. Of course, GA does not occur at every possible turn transition place, just those at which the speaker wishes to display for the recipient that their speaking turn is to be regarded as properly completed, and that the speaker role can now be taken by the recipient.

As was pointed out earlier, there are several ways in which any speaking turn can be extended beyond possible completion points, and it is for this reason that the convention of using GA had to be developed.

In this conversation there is just one transition from one speaker to the other where GA is not used. The resulting confusion appears as a one-line gap in the transcript.

Activity 5.3

For each speaking turn in the telephone conversation:
(a) indicate possible turn transition places with the symbol '+';
(b) indicate whether any turn extensions beyond possible transition places involve:
    (i) Same Activity Addition (SAA),
    (ii) Dependent Activity Addition (DAA), or
    (iii) Independent Activity Addition (IAA).

The following is suggested as a sample analysis of a fragment of the conversation:

Niki	HELLO + GA
Mother-in-law	HI + (IAA) MOM HERE + (IAA) HOW IS NIKI TODAY + GA
Niki	IM FINE + (SAA) MY ARM IS SORE + GA
Mother-in-law	YES + (SAA) THE DOCTOR SAID IT WOULD BE + (IAA) HOW IS YOUR TUMMY + GA
Niki	I THINK IT IS FINE + GA
Mother-in-law	ARE YOU STILL IN PAIN + GA
Niki	NO + (SAA) I DONT HAVE PAIN + GA
Mother-in-law	THAT IS GOOD + (IAA) TELL IAN TO BRING OVER THAT BILL + (SAA) YOU GOT FROM THE BANK + (SAA) AND AN OLD ONE + (SAA) SO I CAN SEE HOW MUCH DIFFERENCE YOU HAVE TO PAY MORE + (DAA) I HAVE TO KNOW HOW MUCH MORE YOU ARE GOING TO HAVE TO PAY THEM + (SAA) SO I KNOW WHAT IM TALKING ABOUT + (SAA) WHEN I CALL THEM + GA

Activity 5.4

Consider the mother-in-law's final speaking turn and note the ways in which SAA commponents are linked together. Pay particular attention to the nature of the grammatical links between the component activities.

Discussion

Link 1: TELL IAN TO BRING OVER THAT BILL +
YOU GOT FROM THE BANK

In this case the link involves the addition of a relative clause which specifies in more detail the particular bill that the mother is referring to. The link would have been even more explicit had the speaker chosen the option of using a relative pronoun such as *which* to introduce the relative clause.

Link 2: YOU GOT FROM THE BANK +
AND AN OLD ONE

In this case the link involves the addition through the use of the conjunction *AND* of a phrase in which the proform *ONE* refers back to earlier material, i.e. the noun phrase *THAT BILL YOU GOT FROM THE BANK*. In other words we must interpret the item *ONE* as having the same meaning as this earlier noun phrase. When we use items like *one, he, she, it* etc. to refer back to earlier material in this way we say that we are using **anaphora** or **anaphoric reference**. The use of anaphoric reference is a crucial means of maintaining links across stretches of talk.

Link 3: AND AN OLD ONE +
SO I CAN SEE HOW MUCH DIFFERENCE YOU
HAVE TO PAY MORE

Here we can see that the form *SO* has been used at the point where a link is made. What the *SO* does is to introduce a clause which provides a reason for the inclusion of an old bill in the request that is being made. Notice that the clause introduced by *SO* does not provide a reason for the request as a whole but simply for a matter that is, as it were, internal to that request considered as a whole. It should not therefore be viewed as a dependent activity addition.

82

Link 4: I HAVE TO KNOW HOW MUCH MORE YOU ARE
GOING TO PAY THEM +
SO I KNOW WHAT IM TALKING ABOUT +

At this point the speaker has moved on to a new activity. The activity is concerned with providing a reason for the request considered as a whole. This first link within this new activity is again accomplished through the use of *SO*. Here it introduces a clause which provides a reason for a matter contained within the preceding clause, i.e. it asserts why she has to know but does not assert why she is saying she has to know.

Link 5: SO I KNOW WHAT IM TALKING ABOUT +
WHEN I CALL THEM

This final link in the speaker's turn is accomplished through the use of the item *WHEN* which introduces a clause that goes on to specify something further about an event which is partly the concern of the preceding SAA. And this event is, of course, the occasion of her talking to someone about something at the bank.

Relative clauses and clauses introduced by items like *so* and *when* i.e. clauses which provide supplementary information, are usually called **subordinate clauses**.

We have seen how speaking turns in the special sort of conversation we have investigated are put together by the speakers, i.e. 'designed' and 'built' using appropriate turn constructional units, and then recognised by the recipient as individual activities or sequences of activities. The speaker seems to have a right to carry on doing his or her chosen activity or activities until he or she chooses to display that the activity or activity sequence is finally complete. The recipient takes this display as a signal to take on the speaking role and, in the case of the conversation we have been investigating, as a signal to start typing.

5.5 Turn-taking and face-to-face interaction

Let's now turn our attention to face-to-face spoken verbal interaction. There is, of course, a wide range of factors that might conceivably have a bearing on how turn-taking is organised in any particular instance of spoken verbal interaction. These can include:

(i) the situation,
(ii) the purpose,
(iii) the number of people involved in the interaction,
(iv) the status or roles that the participants have.

To illustrate how structure and control can be achieved in two different sorts of verbal interaction, we shall now investigate examples of conversations involving just two participants – two-party conversations – a media interview and a conversation between a mother and her daughter.

5.5.1 Activities and turn-taking in the media interview

The media interview was recorded in the 1950s, and involves a female interviewer and a 103-year-old resident of Tunbridge Wells. The interview has the apparent purpose of eliciting reminiscences of Tunbridge Wells for the entertainment of an over-hearing radio audience. These facts suggest the following hypotheses with respect to the structure and control of turn-taking in this interaction:

(i) the predominant activity of the interviewer's turns will be to request information;
(ii) the predominant activity of the interviewee's turns will be to respond with requested information;
(iii) turn transitions only occur at points where these activities are recognisably complete;
(iv) turn transitions only occur at points where the completion of these activities is explicitly signalled.

Activity 5.5 _____

Examine the extract and identify

(i) interviewer turns which do not request information;
(ii) interviewee turns which do not respond with requested information;
(iii) turn transitions which occur at points where an activity is not recognisably complete;

(iv) turn transitions which occur at points where the completion
of an activity is not explicitly signalled.

The media interview – a transcription

A ↑Well↑ now Mr Cranville: ↑you↑ tell me: about ↑Tun↑
bridge We::ˇlls::=

B = I don't know anything about /evərɪts/ Tunbridge Wèlls:
(1.0)

A But you've lived here ↑I believe↑ since you were ↑eigh↑tee::n:=

B = That's righːt:

A And has it cha:nged ↑much↑ in all that ↑ti::me↑

B Ye:s ↑we↑ had a lotta cha:nges:

A What ↑ what's↑ the biggest cha::nge ⌈ do you think ⌉
B   ⌊ well er(.)   ⌋

A lotta building an' (1.5) 's all I:: know about it ↑about↑
Tunbridge Wèlls:
(0.5)

A What's the nicest thing about Tunbridge Wè:lls=

B =What's whàt

A What's the ↑nic↑est thing:: about Tunbridge Wèll⌈ s: ⌉
                                                  ⌊ I ⌋

B don't knoẁ::

A ↑Don't↑ you know ↑any↑ thing ni:ce about it

B Nò

A Nothing at a::ìl:

B No I know nothing about ↑Tun↑ bridge We::ìls:

A But it ↑must↑ be a healthy plá::ce

B ḿm

A It must be a healthy plá::ce=

B = Oh it's a healthy place 'cos you can go ba:ck (.) to the fif-
(.) ↑fif↑tee:nth and ↑six↑teenth century ca::ǹ't you
(1.0)

A Yè::s (.) ↑I↑ know ⌈ any ⌉
B   ⌊ Bet ⌋ you don't know thaːt:
(0.5)

A Oh yes:: ↑I↑ knew thaːt ↑but ⌈ any ⌉ ways↑
B   ⌊ Oh ⌋

A it ↑must↑ be healthy: for you to be:: ˙h ↑look↑ing so
wonderful (.) at this a::ge

B   Well why shouldn't I look wonderful
     (1.0)

A   m̈m (.) ˙h well erm (.) that of course comes from the <u>inner</u>
     spirit ↑I know::↑

B   m̈m

A   <u>That</u> comes from the inner <u>sp</u>irit:
     (1.0)

B   /ɪnsːiɪn⌈ s/ ⌉
A   ⌊ well ⌋ from your ow::n <u>sp</u>irit

B   /sɪtɪn/
     (2.5)

B   I don't know what you wa:nt me to <u>say:</u> if I can say anything
     to <u>please</u> you I ↑wi::ll:↑ but: ˙h

A   What you're saying de↑lights↑ me:=

B   m̈m

A   What you're saying de<u>lights</u> me:⌈ ˙h   ↑I↑ ⌉
B   ⌊ m̈m ⌋

A   want you to tell me something about <u>living</u> in Tunbridge

     We:⌈ lls ⌉
B   ⌊↑W⌋ell↑ I can't tell you ↑I↑ <u>lived</u> in Tunbridge Wells
     that's all I know about ↑it↑
     (2.0)

A   Er (.) ↑tell me↑ t- ↑can↑ you tell me anything about the
     panti::les=

B   =m̈m

A   Can you tell me <u>anything</u> about the <u>pa</u>nti::les:

B   No:ˑ I don't know anything 'bout the pan ↑ti::les:↑ I know
     it's the <u>pantiles</u> that's a:ll I <u>know</u> about it:
     (2.0)

A   Erm and: ↑can↑ you tell me ↑any↑thing: ˙h (.) about changes
     in <u>transport:</u>there: ↑I↑ suppose once upon a time there were
     hor::ses where <u>now</u> there are motor cár::s

B   No I can't tell you anything about that:
     (0.5)

A   You don't <u>remember</u> tha:t

B   Well I dare say I <u>could</u> remember but I didn't have any ˙h
     ↑bus↑ iness in it ↑that's↑ the thing makes you <u>re</u>member
     when ↑you↑ got some <u>money</u> in it::

A Oh::ˆ (.) You'll be a hundred and three:⌈ : the ⌉first of next
B ⌊ Yeah ⌋
A Januar⌈ ÿ (.) ⌉
B ⌊ Ye:s ⌋
A and ↑who::'s↑ coming to the party
B Who's coming to the party (0.5) I don't know well y- •h
  ↑you↑ can come if you could subscribe a b- a ↑fiver↑ •h so as
  we could drink your health (.) could have some co::ffee
A Oh splendid I'⌈ ll ⌉accept the invita:tion::
B ⌊ Y- ⌋
B heheheah (.) he ⌈ he ⌉
A ⌊ •h ⌋So nex- next (.) ↑first↑ of January you'll
⌈ be ⌉ a hundred and ⌈ three ⌉::
B ⌊ Y- ⌋ ⌊ Yes ⌋we should be able to s-
  supp↑ly↑ you with some co::ffee
  (1.5)
A Mr Cranville would you ↑just↑ to finish off tell us your full
  na::me and how old you are now::ˆ
B ṁm
A ↑Just to finish off↑ would you tell us your full name: and
  how old you are now::ˆ
B True naṁe ⌈ my name ⌉
A ⌊ Your ⌋full na:ṁe:
B My full na:ṁe (.) Alfred Cranwell
  (1.5)
A And ↑how↑ old are ↑you:↑
  (1.0)
B Born in eighteen fifty one: (.) first o' January •h and you can
  work that out for your↑self↑ can't you

Discussion

For the most part the interviewer's turns are indeed concerned
with requesting information, but there are occasions where the
interviewer uses a turn to perform some other activity. The
interviewer, for example, uses a turn to respond to a request for
clarification:

Fragment 1

    A   But it ↑<u>must</u>↑ be a <u>healthy</u> pla::ce

    B   mm

→ *A*   It must be a <u>healthy</u> pla::ce

or to comment on a response made by the interviewee in a prior turn:

Fragment 2

→ *A*   ... ↑but anyways↑ it ↑<u>must</u>↑ be healthy: for <u>you</u> to be::
    •h ↑look↑ing so wonderful (.) at this a::ge

or even to respond to what the interviewer takes to be an invitation:

Fragment 3

→ *A*   Oh <u>splen</u>did I'll accept the invita:tion::

Similarly the interviewee's turns are predominantly concerned with dealing with the interviewer's requests for information, albeit not always too successfully. However, we find, for example, that his turns can be used to seek clarification of a prior turn:

Fragment 4

→ *B*   What's what

or to challenge what the interviewee takes to be a particular attitude implied in the prior talk of the interviewer:

Fragment 5

→ *B*   Well why shouldn't I look wonderful

or to make what appears to be, or at least is taken to be, a conditional invitation:

Fragment 6

→ *B*   ... well y- •h ↑you↑ can come if you could <u>subscibe</u> a b-
    a ↑<u>fiver</u>↑ •h so as we could drink your <u>health</u> (.) could
    have some co::ffee

or to offer comment on his own performance:

Fragment 7

→ *B*   I don't know what you wa:nt me to <u>say</u>: if I can say
    anything to <u>please</u> you I ↑wi::ll:↑ but: •h

The first two of our hypotheses would thus seem to be confirmed through our inspection of the data.

Moving on to the third hypothesis, there again seem to be very few instances of turn transition at places other than at the point of recognisable completion of an activity. Where it does occur, then either possible activity completion is recognisably imminent and highly predictable, as in the following instances:

Fragment 8

```
A   What's the ↑nic↑est thing:: about Tunbridge Wèll ⎡ s: ⎤
B                                                     ⎣ I ⎦
    don't knoẅ::
```

Fragment 9

```
A   ˙h So nex- next (.) ↑first↑ of January you'll ⎡ be ⎤ a
B                                                 ⎣ y- ⎦
A   hundred and ⎡ three ⎤ ::
B               ⎣ yes   ⎦
```

or the current speaker passes the possible activity completion point by an extension of the turn through a same activity addition or new activity addition. An example would be:

Fragment 10

```
A   What ↑what's↑ the biggest cha::nge + ⎡ do  you  think ⎤
B                                        ⎣ well er (.)     ⎦
```

So again our third hypothesis would seem to be confirmed and such exceptions as there are can be plausibly explained.

The fourth hypothesis suggested that there would be some explicit display or signal that a recipient could use as a basis for taking up the speaking role at a possible turn completion point. A first problem is to determine what such an explicit signal would be like. There is certainly nothing like the GA symbol used in the typed conversation investigated earlier. Nevertheless, there is some evidence that turn transition occurs when one of two sorts of things happen at the point where an activity is possibly complete. Either the way in which the final word is said, i.e. the **prosodics**, in the performance of the activity is marked in some way, or the turn is extended by an activity whose explicit purpose is to get the recipient to respond.

An example of marked prosodics would be the stretching of the vowel and final consonant, combined with falling pitch on the word *Wells* as it occurs at the point of activity completion in the following example:

Fragment 11

A ↑Well↑ now Mr Granville: ↑you↑ tell me: about ↑Tun↑ bridge We::lls::=

B =

An example of a turn extended by an activity whose explicit purpose is to get the recipient to respond would be the activity done with the words *do you think* in the following:

Fragment 12

A What ↑what's↑ the biggest cha::nge ⌈ do you think ⌉
B   ⌊ well er (.) ⌋
     (.) lotta building an' (1.5)

In this example the main activity of the turn is completed with the word *change*. The word is produced with the stressed syllable stretched and with falling pitch. Although the interviewee attempts to accomplish a turn transition at this point, the current turn holder, i.e. the interviewer, opts to extend the turn with an explicit invitation to respond.

Do you think

Actual turn transition is accomplished only after this additional activity of the interviewer is accomplished.

Thus, it seems that prosodic marking can be overridden as a signal for turn transition by the very person who produces it. It can be overridden simply by the speaker opting to go on to do an additional activity. We should also note that the explicit signalling of places for turn transition is not necessary for the transition to occur successfully, i.e. without much of a pause and without much overlap. There are many instances of such transitions in the data under investigation.

What this suggests is that the actual point of turn transition is in the control of the current speaker. However, the ultimate instrument of control is not the use of explicit signalling. Rather it seems to be a mutually acknowledged set of rights and obligations. What this amounts to is the right of the speaker to hold a turn until any projected activity is completed. Conversely, a recipient has an obligation not to take a turn whilst a current speaker is engaged in the performance of some activity.

The knack of holding on to a turn is then to initiate an additional activity before a recipient initiates a turn. And the knack of getting a turn is to start one before a current speaker can initiate an additional activity.

Of course, the set of rights and obligations relevant to the control of turn-taking can be abused. For example, a recipient might initiate an activity before a speaker's projected activity is completed, or even before its imminent completion could be predicted. When this happens we have a case of overlapping talk that is interruptive, i.e. an **interruption**:

Fragment 13

  A Ye::s (.) ↑I↑ know ⌈ any- ⌉
  B   ⌊ Bet ⌋ you don't know tha:t:

People, of course, can interrupt each other for all sorts of reasons. Here the interruption probably occurs because the interviewee wants to make the most of the display of knowledge produced in his immediately prior turn. The opportunity to do so would no doubt be lost if the interviewer completed a new activity which might well require the interviewee to respond in some particular way.

So it seems that our fourth hypothesis is not confirmed by the data. Explicit signalling is not necessary for effective transfer of speaking turns. What is necessary is the mutual acknowledgement of a set of speaker rights and recipient obligations. Explicit signalling can contribute to the management of turn transfer and will probably be used by people who have assumed a particular responsibility for, or have a professional responsibility for, ensuring a smooth flow to the talk within an interaction.

Activity 5.6 _____

Consider who would be most likely to explicitly signal points of turn transfer in the following interactional situations:

- adult stranger conversing with a small child
- teacher with a large class
- a job interview
- a police interrogation
- a chat show

- a couple at breakfast
- conversation with an old person

Activity 5.7

Identify which participant in the media interview uses explicit signalling to the greatest extent, and what signalling methods are used.

5.5.2 Activities and turn-taking in a domestic argument

The second interaction we shall look at is a conversation between a mother and her daughter. The topic of conversation is the mother's other daughter. There is a history of stongly held difference of opinion between the two participants about the mother's behaviour towards the other daughter. The mother sees her behaviour as supportive, whilst her daughter sees the 'supportive' behaviour as overindulgent. Given this history and the current conversational topic, what hypotheses are suggested with respect to the turn-taking of the interaction? I would suggest the following:

(i)   Each participant is likely to take any opportunity to express their own views (each has strong reasons be in the speaker role but only weak reasons to be in the listener role);
(ii) neither participant will acknowledge the rights of the other as a speaker but rather each will compete for the speaking turn by interrupting the other to have their say.

To test these hypotheses we could try to find out just where in the flow of talk the two participants attempt to speak and whether there is any evidence that either participant at any points in the talk actually acknowledges that they have actually interrupted the other participant. Let's first investigate where in the flow of talk the participants attempt to get their speaking turns.

Activity 5.8

Identify in the conversation between the mother and her daughter instances where a participant has attempted to take the speaker role at a point that turns out to have been too early.

The conversation between a mother and daughter – a transcription

M Your father and I were talking this morning wh- (.) and
↑we said↑ that when ↑you::↑ (.) get married (.) and have a
home of your own: (.) ↑you're↑ going to be nice and
strong:: (.) you'll be able to ↑co:pe↑ on your ↑own↑ (.)
⎡ you'll ⎤
D ⎣ I will ⎦

M You'll k⎡eep the place ↑really spotless↑ ⎤
D   ⎣ I will I'll make my friends   ⎦

M ⎡ and you'll ⎤ make
D ⎣ I'll make ⎦   friends

M Well we said all this because you're a very strong
character:: (.)

D Al⎡ right ⎤
M   ⎣ ↑Kren ⎦ isn't↑

D But Mum wha- ↑what would she do if none of us lived in
Reading an-↑ or if she had to get a house out of Reading
↑what↑ would she do::⎡ you tell me then ⎤
M   ⎣ She would ha-   ⎦ (.)

   She would have to man ⎡ age: ⎤
D   ⎣ Ex   ⎦ actly so why don't
   ⎡ she star ⎤t
M ⎣ Ye:s   ⎦

D trying to ⎡ now:: ⎤ (.)
M   ⎣ But   ⎦ the poi⎡nt is she's ↑not such
D   ⎣ but not she can't because
   you sympathise with her ⎤
M a strong::↑   ⎦ character

D •h•h•h ↑It's not the point↑ she's as str- ↑she↑ stronger than
what she makes out::: I tell you now

M Well ↑may↑ be ⎡ ::   ⎤(.) ⎡ maybe   ⎤
D   ⎣ Sh e's a ⎣ lot strong- ⎦ ↑cos↑ otherwise I
would have drived her mad when she lived here but no
she's a lot stronger than what she makes out to you lot I'll
tell you that now:

M Well I'm just trying to help her get ⎡ (.) acc ⎤ limatised(.)
D   ⎣ Yeah   ⎦

M ⎡ ˙h˙h so ↑therefore↑ ⎤
D ⎣ Exactly you helped her ⎦
M I've tried to ⎡ do it ↑grad↑ually::   ⎤
D   ⎣ You ↑helped↑ her when she ⎦
come <u>here</u> you helped her when she come here ˙h˙h then
you had to help in doing <u>other</u> things when she was here
˙h˙h then you ↑hel↑ ped her in summat else then summat
else then summat else ˙h˙h now she's gone you're helping
in summat else ↑again↑ =
M   ⎡ jus- ⎤
D = Well I'm ⎣ ˙h˙h ⎦↑then↑ it'd be <u>summat</u> else and <u>summat</u>
<u>else</u> and <u>summat</u> <u>else</u> (.) but in the long run you ain't going
to help 'cos she's going to be lo::st
(0.5)
M ↑Well↑ then:: ↑I↑ then I've done all I can haven't
  ⎡ I I've got the satisfaction of knowing I've ⎤
D ⎣ <u>Exactly</u> now you needn't bother any more ⎦
M tried
D You <u>have</u> tried (.) ↑<u>you've</u>↑ tried more than anyone
  ⎡ could ⎤
M ⎣ Right ⎦
D try
M So now I'm grad⎡ ually trying to break her ⎤ off
D   ⎣ Now you should give up ⎦
M coming up so often =
D = Exactly because you might as well give ↑u::p↑
M Well why have ↑why↑ should I give up
D Because:: (.) you ain't ↑helping↑ ⎡ her no more   ⎤
M   ⎣ DID I GIVE UP ⎦
ON YOU
D Don't bother:: ↑I↑ don't need your help though
(0.5)
M ⎡ No but as I say it's ↑nice↑ to have ↑<u>people</u> there↑ ⎤
D ⎣ That's the trouble with you lot you're too soft ⎦
on her (.) the <u>more</u>:: you lot are like that the <u>worse</u> she's
going to be::
(1.0)
It's Karen all ↑over↑ she know she got it coming cushy she
ain't got the <u>bother</u> have she::

Discussion

You will certainly have found many places in this conversation where a participant begins to speak before the other participant has actually completed what it was that she had to say in the course of her speaking turn. Indeed, it turns out that every transfer of speaking turn occurs with some degree of overlap involved.

On the face of it this would seem to confirm the hypothesis that the participants' primary concern in this interaction is to occupy the speaker role. But does this mean that the participants simply begin to speak whenever the fancy takes them without any regard for any system in their turn-taking behaviour?

To answer this last question we could look at the precise places in the talk where overlap occurs to see if their placement really is haphazard, as would be expected if no regard were being paid to any system for turn-taking, or if their placement seems to follow some sort of pattern. The existence of such a pattern could be established if it could be shown that the points of overlap shared certain features in common.

The idea of turn constructional units would seem to be useful here. Turns are built out of turn constructional units which are the linguistic means we use to accomplish the activities we use our speaking turns for. Now turn constructional units can be words, phrases, clauses or combinations of clauses. Whatever sort of linguistic item any particular constructional unit happens to be its purpose is to contribute to the accomplishment of some dependent or independent activity in the course of a speaking turn. As we saw earlier it seems that a speaker has a right to the speaker role up to the point at which the utterance of a turn constructional unit that is being used in the accomplishment of an activity is complete. When such a turn constructional unit is heard as complete and the speaker has not indicated that there will be a continuation through SAA, DAA, or IAA then other participants have a right to the speaker role. (See Activity 5.3.)

So with the conversation under investigation we could look to see if there is any regular relationship between the places where overlap begins, **onset of overlap**, and the completion of turn constructional units by the participant already in speaker role.

Activity 5.9

Consider the following instances of overlap and discuss the relationship between onset of overlap and the turn constructional unit currently in progress.

Fragment 1

M You'll k⌈eep the place ↑really spotless↑ ⌉
    ⌊I will I'll make my friends   ⌋

Fragment 2

M She would have to man ⌈age: ⌉
D   ⌊Ex ⌋actly so why don't she start

Fragment 3

M Well we said all this because you're a very strong character:: (.)

D Al ⌈right   ⌉
    ⌊↑Karen isn't↑⌋

Discussion

In the first fragment the onset of the overlapping talk is at a point just after the current speaker has pronounced the first consonant of the main verb of a clause. It is impossible at this point to predict what the verb will be and so impossible to decide what contribution the turn constructional unit of which it is a part will make to the activity being accomplished in the speaking turn. In this case then it would seem that the overlap is indeed haphazard.

In the second fragment the onset of overlapping talk is again at a point where the pronunciation of the main verb is incomplete. It occurs just after the current speaker has pronounced the first syllable of the verb. However, in this case there is more of a possibility that the identity of the verb can be predicted and indeed that the activity being accomplished by the turn constructional unit in which it occurs can be predicted.

This is because the mother's speaking turn at this point is in fact a response to a particular sort of question posed by the daughter. The daughter, through her question, has in effect challenged the mother to acknowledge what, for the daughter at least, is obvious, i.e. that in the absence of support the other daughter will have to manage on her own. The possible completion of the mother's turn constructional unit is thus highly predictable and the completion of the first syllable serves to confirm that prediction. It provides just enough material to enable the daughter to feel secure in behaving as if the mother will indeed produce the word *manage* in responding to her challenge and so be responding in the way set up and anticipated.

This confirmation provides the daughter with a basis for anticipating turn completion and so with a basis for initiating her own turn at speaking. There is what might be termed a **preemptive start**. So the onset of the overlapping talk is not haphazard but can be seen to be related to the recognition of a point of possible completion of a turn constructional unit.

In the third fragment the onset of overlapping talk occurs on completion of the first syllable of the word *alright*. What seems to have happened here is that the mother has completed a turn constructional unit with the word *character* which is stretched and then followed by a micropause. That this is the possible completion point of a turn constructional unit arises because the word occurs in clause final position. The daughter thus has very strong grounds for assuming that the mother will not be continuing in the speaker role. However, just as the daughter initiates her turn the mother simultaneously produces what is a SAA. This extension of the turn could not have been predicted so again we can see that there is a basis for the initiation of a new speaking turn. There is what might be termed a **simultaneous start**. The overlap is thus not haphazard but can be accounted for by reference to there being grounds for assuming or predicting completion of turn constructional units.

Activity 5.10

Examine all instances of overlap in the conversation and decide which are haphazard and which can be accounted for by reference to there being grounds for assuming or predicting completion of turn constructional units.

Discussion

You should have found that there is indeed a pattern to the occurrence of overlap. In the majority of cases there are grounds for assuming or predicting turn constructional unit completion. It is only where this is not the case that we can properly speak of **competitive interruption**. Otherwise the overlaps are to be regarded as either preemptive or simultaneous starts.

So even in a conversation such as this where the participants have a high degree of emotional commitment to the topic at hand and where they have every reason to be in the speaker rather than the listener role we find that the considerable pressure on speaking turns does not result in a lot of competitive interruption. Such overlap as does occur occurs as a product of, rather than in spite of, the operation of a system for turn-taking.

Let's now try and establish whether the participants at any point actually acknowledge that they have interrupted the other participant with their talk. Such acknowledgement could either be explicit or implicit. Explicit acknowledgement would involve doing things like making apologies and saying such things as:

> Sorry. I didn't mean to butt in.

Implicit acknowledgement would involve doing such things as behaving as if one's overlapping talk should be ignored – it occurred when it shouldn't have and therefore should be treated as if it hadn't. One way of having one's overlapping talk treated in this way is simply to repeat it when it will no longer be in overlap, i.e. when it is in the clear. The repetition amounts to an acknowledgement that the first attempt was illegitimate because someone else's talk was in progress, now here is the legitimate attempt.

The conversation we are investigating has no explicit acknowledgements of interruption but there may well be some implicit acknowledgements. And if there are such acknowledgements then this will show that the hypothesis that participants disregard the rights of speakers in this kind of highly charged argument in conversation cannot be confirmed.

Activity 5.11 _____

Identify repetitions of overlapping talk in the conversation that can be regarded as implicit acknowledgements of interruption.

Example

D ⎡ You tell me then ⎤
M ⎣ She would ha- ⎦ (.) She would have to manage:

Discussion

Following a simultaneous start with the daughter who is the current speaker, the mother repeats her overlapped talk when she is in the clear, i.e. when it is more or less obvious that the daughter has finished.

6. Taking turns in multi-party talk

6.1 Introduction

So far we have looked at conversations involving just two participants and have found that people take turns in an orderly way. This we have seen to be the case in both highly formal media interviews and in spontaneous family arguments. We shall now investigate the organisation of turn-taking in cases where there are more than two participants.

We shall be concentrating on how turn-taking can be structured and controlled in such multi-party conversations. Consider, for example, the BBC television programme *Question Time*. In this programme members of an invited studio audience are invited to put questions of current topical interest to a panel of four guests chosen for their prominence in public life. Now it's possible that the guests could simply mingle with the audience, answering questions as they arose. But, of course, this would hardly serve the purpose of the programme, which is to entertain an onlooking audience of millions of television viewers.

Panel and audience have to be so arranged that camera crews and their equipment can take appropriate shots of current speakers. This problem is solved by placing the panel in a semi-circular arrangement facing the studio audience. With an audience of a hundred or so people, each possibly wanting to ask a question, one can imagine that competition to get a hearing for a question could be intense and easily result in a noisy clamour for attention. At the same time people who are prominent in public life generally have an axe to grind on just about any issue of public interest. How, then, can their 'axe-grinding' be limited in a programme that only lasts for an hour?

The answer is, of course, to have a chairperson who all must agree has the right to determine who will speak, how long they will speak for, what they will speak about and the relevance of what they say when they do speak. For the programme *Question Time* this role used to be taken for many years by Sir Robin Day, a man of strong personality who styled himself the 'Grand Inquisitor'. His presence ensured a pattern of turn-taking and participant contribution that was explicitly structured and centrally controlled. Questions are put 'through' the chair and it is the chairperson who gets particular participants to make contributions on the designated topics. All the participants do is to make contributions as and when requested to do so.

6.2 Taking turns when there are more than two

The interaction we shall investigate here is a more casual but nevertheless focused conversation between four adults, three male and one female. The adults are colleagues of equal status and they have been asked to talk specifically on the topic 'Learning to drive'. The speakers sit facing each other in easy chairs with no one else present. These facts suggest the following hypotheses with respect to the structure and control of turn-taking and participant contribution within this interaction:

(i)   each participant is likely to be in both listener and speaker role in the course of the interaction:

(ii) when in the listener role a participant can be more or less active in this role and the level of involvement as an active listener will be signalled by the listener's use of so-called **back-channel** behaviour such as *yes, mm, oh really, quite* or more extended expressions of appreciation or acknowledgement;

(iii)   as they take on the speaker role, i.e. when they are doing more than back-channels, appreciations, acknowledgements etc. all participants will use their turns either to get someone else to say something on the designated topic or to say something themselves on the designated topic;

(iv)   participants' contributions will involve sustained narratives, usually accounts of their own relevant experiences, delivered in speaking turns that extend over several possible completion points;

(v)   participants will have to compete for what will inevitably be limited opportunities for speaking turns in which to make their own contributions or to get others to make contributions;

(vi)   participants will probably be more interested in what one participant might have to say rather than another at a given point so sometimes participants will encourage one participant's contribution over another's.

Activity 6.1 _____

Examine the following extract and:

(i)   identify the pattern of alternation between participants – the pattern could be expressed as A:B:A:C:B:A:C:B:D etc.

(ii)   identify who is mostly in the speaker role and who is most active when in the listener role;

(iii)   describe how speakers get their contributions into the conversation;

(iv)   for each participant select an extended turn and show the types of extension involved, i.e. SAA, DAA, IAA;

(v)   identify instances of apparent competition for an opportunity to speak;

(vi)   identify instances where a speaker controls the transfer of a speaking turn in such a way that a specific contribution from a specific participant is ensured.

Learning to drive – a transcription

A   I'm just <u>teach</u>ing:: (.) <u>two</u> of my daughters to dri:ve (.) ↑one's↑ already got a provisional licence ↑cos she's seventeen:::↑ (.) ↑the other's↑ sixteen so she can't get a provisional licence until her <u>birth</u>day (.) ˙h so:: (.) with <u>her</u> the <u>young</u>est <u>Sarah</u> (.) we have to go to a big <u>car</u> park at

the s̲upermarket: (.) we just d̲r̲i̲v̲e̲ around t̲h̲e̲r̲e̲ (.) but it's
↑quite↑ useful ↑I mean:↑ (.) she can get to know the
ba:sics ⌈ there ⌉

B ⌊ mm ⌋ (.) °That's ⌈ right ⌉°
C ⌊ sounds ⌋ quite

↑d̲a̲n̲g̲e̲r̲o̲u̲s̲↑ to me
(0.5)

A ↑Well↑ it i̲s̲ ⌈ because ⌉ ↑e̲v̲e̲r̲y̲b̲o̲d̲y̲ goes the::re and
C ⌊ do you do it ⌋

A yh˙h˙hehes⌈ ::↑ ⌉
B ⌊ Is ⌋ it actually ↑legal↑ (.) on a car park

A ↑Well↑ er yeah (.) it is because you're:: ↑you're↑ not
actually:: (.) er you ↑know↑ (.) o̲n̲:̲:̲ (.) the p̲ublic
h̲i̲g̲h̲way:: (.) and t̲h̲e̲r̲e̲f̲o̲r̲e̲:̲ ⌈ (.) ⌉
B ⌊ mm ⌋

A it ma̲ý̲:̲ be that you shouldn't be on ↑their↑ premises: (.) er
but:: (.) you ↑cer↑ tainly don't need to have a l̲icence to
dri::ve on:: ⌈ (.) ⌉ you know (.) ⌈ places ⌉ like that ↑you
B ⌊ mm ⌋ ⌊ mm ⌋

get::↑ (.)

A y̲o̲u̲n̲g̲ k̲ids driving f̲a̲r̲m̲ t̲r̲actors on far::ms for example
⌈ (.) ⌉
B ⌊ True ⌋

A ⌈ because they're ⌉ ↑they're↑ n̲o̲t̲ on /ðiː/ (.) the public
B ⌊ ye::s ⌋

high:way

D Ever ↑taught↑ anybody e̲lse: (.) to dri:ve

A ˙h˙ well I ↑trie::d↑ to t̲e̲a̲c̲h̲ my wi:fe ↑but↑ t̲h̲a̲t̲ wasn't t̲o̲o̲
successful (.) it's ↑it's↑ working r̲e̲a̲::sonably well with:: (.)
the g̲i̲r̲l̲s̲ and it ↑worked↑ (.) q̲u̲i̲t̲e̲ well with my eldest s̲o̲n̲:̲:̲
(.) you know I ↑I↑ taught h̲i̲m̲

D ↑What↑ was the frustration with your wi̲:fe then

A ↑Well↑ I think she was v̲e̲r̲y̲ unwilling /tu::/ (.) he˙hhe˙h
D ⌈ in any sen ⌉ se o:b̲e̲y̲ ⌈ me ⌉
B ⌊ was she sl- ⌋ ⌊ he ˙h˙ ⌋ e ˙he ˙he ˙he ˙he ˙h ˙h

⌈ ˙h ˙h ⌉
D ⌊ ↑So↑ w̲h̲a̲t̲ ⌋ proc̲edures do you u::se then when ⌈ y- ⌉
A ⌊ ˙h ⌋

↑when↑ you t̲e̲a̲c̲h̲ ⌈ someone ⌉
A ⌊ ↑Well↑ ⌋ with R– (.) with ↑/ðiː/↑

(.) ↑my↑ <u>children</u> it's worked quite well ↑what↑ I tended to do is:: (.) ↑just↑ in our: <u>drive or</u> a <u>car</u>:: park •h <u>teach</u> them the absolute <u>basic</u> things: ↑like↑ <u>clutch</u> control: (.) because ↑I↑ always feel that the most im<u>por</u>:tant thing is to be able to control ↑just↑ that moment when the ↑<u>clutch</u>↑

D   [comes in]
      [To (.)] <u>balance</u> it =

A = Yeah [(.)   ] ↑once↑ you can do <u>that</u>: (.) so that you
D   [↑yeah↑]

can :: s-

A <u>s::et off</u> <u>smoo::thly</u>:: [(.)] and <u>change</u> gear [(.)] then: (.)
D   [mm]   [mm]

A ↑<u>ev</u>↑ everything else more or less follows=
D = Ye s::
C You must have a (.) very long dri::ve
A ↑ Well:: ↑ (.) it's:: 1- ↑long↑ enough:: to be able /tu::/ (.) you know (.) practi [se <u>that</u>   ] <u>one</u> <u>thing</u>:: ↑which↑ I think is
B   [•hu •hu •h]

A [the most <u>basic</u> skill] you nee:d
B [h •eh •e ↑haha↑   ]

B •h•h•h [↑I↑   ]
D   [↑It's] quite↑ a <u>distance</u> though i- ↑<u>in</u>↑ to Castle Howard isn't it

A •ha [h•ah•ah•ah•ah•ah•a]
B   [h•ah•ah•a (.)   ] [*coughs*]

(1.0)

B I think my <u>father</u> would agree with you ↑I remember↑ when <u>I</u> was learning to dri::ve ↑he↑ was on this <u>same</u> idea

   [of] <u>balancing</u>
A [ye:s]

B the clutch •h•h but <u>I</u> hadn't worked out (.) the <u>niceties</u> of steering [(.)] •h and <u>we</u> had a dri::ve that was
A   [yes]

↑perhaps↑ (.)

B ° I don't kn-↑I↑ don't know <u>how</u> long it was ° ↑but↑ the i:dea was <u>I</u> would start at the <u>bottom</u> ↑not↑ facing

roa [d (.)] [and]
A   [Ye:s] [   ]
D   [mm]

B I'd go up the dri::ve ᵒh but he <u>hadn't</u> allow:ed for the <u>fact</u>
that I might end up in the ro:se bed ⌈ (.) which I ⌉ quite
A   ⌊ hᵒehᵒehᵒ   ⌋
genuinely did
B ⌈ (.) ⌉ one day: ⌈ ᵒ and he was ⌉ not happy ᵒ
A ⌊ Yes ⌋   ⌊ mm(.)mm(.)yes ⌋
A Yes
D mh ᵒmh ᵒmh ᵒ
C ⌈ O-   ⌉
B ⌊ ᵒ B ⌋u::t ᵒ
C ↑One↑ thing we don't have in our driving <u>tests</u>:: (.) which I
think they have in some Euro<u>pean</u> countries is a (.) ↑a↑
<u>theory</u> examina:tion=
A = Ye::s (.) ⌈ <u>very</u> ⌉⌈ hit ⌉⌈ and ⌉ miss are theories =
B   ⌊ mm   ⌋⌊ (.) ⌋⌊ mm ⌋
C = It <u>see:ms</u>: (.) yeah I don't know:: (.) <u>what</u> people think
about that:
A I've known people:: (.) b- b- ↑<u>nor</u>↑mally they just ask you:
say four questions on the highway code don't they=
C = mm
A ⌈ and ⌉ I've known people get a:ll four:: <u>wrong</u>:: (.)
B ⌊ Ye:s ⌋
A ⌈ and still be passed ⌉ ⌈ (.) ⌉ because they've ⌈ (.) ⌉ ↑you
B ⌊ And sitll pass   ⌋ ⌊ mm ⌋   ⌊ mm ⌋
know↑ done well enough on
A ⌈ /ð̥ː/ ⌉
B ⌊ mm ⌋
D What (.) <u>here</u> you mean=
A = Yeah (.) ⌈ i- ⌉ in Eng ⌈ land ⌉ (.) yes
B   ⌊ mm ⌋   ⌊ mm   ⌋
C But in er ↑in↑ other countries you have to:: ↑it's↑ like er
(.) ↑an↑ <u>O</u> level <u>exam</u> ↑you↑ have to <u>sit</u> in an examina
  ⌈ tion room ⌉ ↑an::d↑ go ⌈ through:: ⌉⌈ (.)   ⌉
B ⌊ ooh Ye::s ⌋   ⌊ <u>exam</u> ⌋⌊ conditions ⌋
C ⌈ half an hour   ⌉
B ⌊ and ↑ev↑erything ⌋⌈ isn't it ⌉
A   ⌊ Sure   ⌋
B mm
A Yes::

D ˙h ↑I↑ think there ought to be a period (.) ↑immediately↑
after somebody's taken the test (.) ↑even↑ if they pass:ed
where they get erm (.) ↑preferenti- ↑no- not preferential ˙h
some special designation (.) as having just <u>passed</u> the tes::t
so that people ⌈ are ⌉ (.) could be ⌈ care::ful ⌉⌈ when ⌉
B   ⌊ They ⌋ (.)   ⌊ ↑they↑ do ⌋⌊ ˙ ⌋
A   yes

  ⌈ they've ⌉
B   ⌊ ye::s ⌋ ↑ they
B do ↑ that in France:
A You <u>have</u> to keep your <u>L</u> plates on or something like
<u>that</u> for a- ⌈ ↑nother↑ ⌉ couple of ⌈ <u>months</u> ⌉ so that er
B   ⌊ mm ⌋   ⌊ mm ⌋
⌈ (.) there is ⌉ some warn⌈ ing ⌉ in <u>France</u> you spend the
⌊ In <u>Fran</u>- ⌋   ⌊ ye::s ⌋
first <u>year</u>:: (.) with /ð::/ sticker that says <u>ni::nety</u> ⌈ (.) ⌉ on
A   ⌊ mm ⌋
the back ⌈ of the ⌉ car :: ⌈ (.)   ⌉ and you're
          ⌊ <u>Ye</u>::s ⌋   ⌊ that's right ⌋
B not allowed to go faster than ni:⌈ :nety ⌉ (.) ⌈ kilometres ⌉
A   ⌊ Sure ⌋   ⌊   ⌋
D   ↑Can I↑
↑can I↑ jus::t ask you i- i- ↑com↑ing <u>back</u> John
⌈ to   ⌉ the <u>act</u>⌈ ual ⌉
A ⌊ ˙mh˙m ⌋   ⌊ Yes ⌋
D procedure that you u::se when you teach ⌈ some ⌉ body to
A   ⌊ Yes: ⌋
drive ↑yo-↑
D you ↑get↑⌈ (.) ⌉ them going up and down your:: dri::ve
A   ⌊ ˙h ⌋
A Well ↑I↑ get them (.) ↑I↑ get the car <u>flat</u>:: (.) show them
how to switch it on with the car in neutral: (.) get them to
<u>put</u> the car in <u>gear</u>: (.) to start bringing the clutch ↑<u>up</u>↑
<u>just</u> to the point where the car begins to move and then to
put it <u>down</u> again: (.) ⌈ and ⌉ then to bring it up <u>just</u> till it
D   ⌊ mm ⌋
moves again and put it
A ⌈ down ⌉ down again ↑so↑ that they <u>know</u>:: (.) that <u>that</u> is::
D ⌊ Yeah ⌋
(.) <u>how</u>

A   The car actually sets off:: =
D   = Just ↑get↑ ting the f-feet used to that ⌈ (.)   ⌉ balnce::
A   ⌊ Yes get ⌋ ting the
    f-foot used to the point at which the clutch is going to take
    ⌈ up ⌉ ˙h and
D   ⌊ mm ⌋
A   ↑then↑ eventually (.) to actually:: (.) to actually bring it
    up: (.) drive a few yards and then put it down again and
    put the bra:ke on: (.) ↑er↑ because obviously I think
    that the most important thing is h˙h˙ that they should
    ⌈ know ⌉ how to stop it::
D   ⌊ S::top ⌋
A   h˙eh˙eh˙e˙h ˙h˙h an::d and then for example having done
    that a few times:: ↑just↑ in the dri::ve ˙h take the car to this
    big car park where they can (.) ↑hav↑ ing you know
    brought the clutch actually drive round (.) say once:: (.) in
    first gear: (.) the whole way::
D   Yes::
A   and then:: (.) ↑maybe↑ a couple of times more in first
    ↑gear↑ and then try moving into second on one occasion ˙h
    (.) but as I say if the car park's totally empty that's fi:ne
    ⌈ (.) ⌉ but
B   ⌊ mm ⌋
A   occ↑as↑ionally you get three or four:: (.) ↑e↑qually (.)
    beginner (.) beginning:: learner ⌈ s::   ⌉ (.) there together: (.)
B   ⌊ mm ⌋
    h˙ and that
A   can be a bit: (.) ⌈ well   ⌉ ↑act↑ ually there's one point
D   ⌊ Do you ⌋
A   at which there's a drop and ↑I↑ once saw:: somebody
    driving a Cortina ˙h straight o:ver this:: (.) drop of about a
    foot and a hal::f ↑it just↑ sort of (.) did an enormous
    bounce into the air::
C   Christ
A   Very nasty
D   ↑Do you do↑ erm (.) reversing
    (0.5)
A   Well I did ⌈ with my son ⌉ I haven't⌈ got ⌉ to that (.) yeah I
D   ⌊ hill starts ⌋ (.)   ⌊ or ⌋

A haven't quite er ↑hill↑ starts I've done (.) cos my:: <u>e</u>lder
daughter now:: I was gonna say ↑she's↑ <u>got</u> a provisional
licence: (.) and so:: (.) we've driven to Halifax and back
from <u>Leeds</u> for example (.) ↑she's↑ at <u>that</u> sort of stage:

B ⌈ (.) ⌉ but I <u>haven't</u> actually taught her to reverse round
     ⌊ mm ⌋

A corners:⌈ (.) ⌉ I thought it was better to just do some straight-
D   ⌊ mm ⌋

A forward (.) driving steering changing gear and so on
B ↑When your son↑ was learning to drive (.) ↑did↑ he have
any:: (.) <u>les</u>sons with:: /ðiː/ (.) <u>driving schools:</u>

A To <u>get</u> to the <u>test</u> stage (.) yes he he ⌈ booked ⌉ a set of
B   ⌊ That ⌋

A fi::⌈ ve ⌉
B   ⌊ ye: ⌋ s

A ↑⌈ but↑ I think my young daughter⌉ will do the sa ⌈ ::me ⌉
B   ⌊ that's what I was wondering ⌋   ⌊ mm ⌋

A Yeah
B mm

A I think you nee::d to because :: (.) •h I ↑I↑ think what
<u>dri::</u>ving (.) instructors do:: is ↑not just↑ (.) <u>teach</u> you to
<u>drive</u> but teach how to ⌈ pass your driving <u>tes:t</u> ⌉
B   ⌊ Teach you to pass the test ⌋ (.) mm

Discussion

(i) *The pattern of speaker/listener alternation*

In theory it should be possible for an A:B:C:D:A:B:C:D:A:B:
C:D-type pattern to emerge. In this case each participant would
be getting the same opportunities to speak. But in practice rather
different patterns are evident. What seems to be happening is
that there are stretches of talk in which just two participants of
the four alternate as the speakers. It's as if the conversation can
be broken down into a series of exchanges involving just two
participants – such two-party exchanges are referred to as **dyadic**.

This can be seen to be happening, of course, because one party
will be responding to the immediately prior turn and the immediately prior turn will in its turn be responding to its immediately
prior turn. And the majority of turns produced in this way will

be designed with the producer of the turn to which it is a response as its intended recipient. This will inevitably create difficulties for other participants who are not part of the dyad but who want to break into the conversation. We experience this difficulty as the familiar feeling of being left out of a conversation.

(ii) *Predominant speaker/active listener*

The participant who is the predominant speaker is clearly participant A. It is A who is most frequently involved in dyadic exchanges and it is A who in the course of these exchanges has the most extended speaking turns.

Active listenership, on the other hand, can be seen in the use of minimal responses such as *mm*, *yeah* and the like, preemptive turn completions and requests for clarification of matters contained within the immediately prior speaker's contribution. The following are examples of each type of active listenership display contained within the same fragment of talk:

Fragment 1

```
      A  I've known people:: (.) b- b- ↑nor↑mally they just ask
         you: say four questions on the highway code don't
         they =
→   C  = mm                                    (minimal response)
      A  ⌈ And ⌉ I've known people get a:ll four::
→   B  ⌊ ye::s ⌋                               (minimal response)
      A  wrong:: (.)⌈ and still be passed ⌉
→   B            ⌊ and still pass       ⌋      (preemptive turn
                                                   completion)
      A  ⌈ (.) ⌉ because they've ⌈ (.) ⌉ ↑you know↑
→   B  ⌊ mm ⌋                ⌊ mm ⌋            (minimal response)
      A  done well enough on ⌈ /ði:/ ⌉
→   B                       ⌊ mm    ⌋          (mininal response)
→   D  What (.) here you mean                  (clarification request)
```

Taking the conversation as a whole this sort of behaviour is most clearly evident in the participation of B and D. D's active listenership is more localised than B's so that overall it is B who is most active in the listener role.

(iii) *Participant contributions*

To illustrate how one might analyse how particular contributions are constructed and fitted in I shall examine two from speaker A. It soon becomes clear from a survey of A's talk that contributions can come about in two ways. We can distinguish between those that are initiated by the individual who makes the contribution and those that are initiated through the activity of another individual, e.g. through explicit questioning. The first sort of contribution we can call 'self-initiated' and the second sort 'other-initiated'.

Contribution I: self-initiated, describing speaker's recent experience of teaching his children to drive.

Fragment 2

→　*A*　I'm just teaching:: (.) two of my daughters to dri:ve (.)
　　　↑one's↑ already got a provisional licence ↑cos she's
　　　seventeen:::↑ (.) ↑the other's↑ sixteen so she can't get a
　　　provisional licence until her birthday (.) •h so:: (.) with
　　　her the youngest Sarah (.) we have to go to a big car
　　　park at the supermarket: (.) we just drive around there
　　　(.) but it's ↑quite↑ useful ↑I mean:↑ (.) she can get to
　　　know the ba:sics there

In this instance the problem of fitting the contribution in is really one of getting talk on the designated topic of the conversation started. Whatever the participant says will have to display some relatedness to 'Learning to drive' but that relatedness could be of any sort. It could include the organisation of driving schools, traffic laws, the history of the automobile and its impact on social life or a host of other matters. What this participant chooses to do, though, as the first contributor on the designated topic, is to recount recent personal experience. No subsequent contribution will be made with such freedom, because all subsequent contributions will have to be fitted in with what has gone before.

One particular way in which the speaker signals the relatedness of the several facts expressed in this first contribution to the designated topic is through the use of various ways of referring to things already mentioned earlier in the turn. This activity of referring back is known as **anaphoric reference** (see page 82) and it is a very important method that speakers use to achieve **cohesion** in their talk. In fragment 2, for example, notice the different ways in which the speaker's children are referred to, having been introduced as *two of my daughters, one, she, the other, the youngest Sarah.*

Contribution II: other-initiated, commenting on the legality of under-age driving on other than public roads.

Fragment 3

→ B   Is it actually ↑legal↑ (.) on a car park

A   ↑Well↑ er yeah (.) it is because you're:: ↑you're↑ not
actually:: (.) er you ↑know↑ (.) on:: (.) the public
highway:: (.) and therefore: [(.)]
B   [mm]

A   it may: be that you shouldn't be on ↑their↑ premises: (.)
er but:: (.) you ↑cer↑ tainly don't need to have a licence
to dri::ve on:: [(.)] you know (.) [places]
B   [mm]   [mm] places like
that ↑you get::↑ (.)

A   young kids driving farm tractors on far::ms for example
[(.)]
B   ⌊ true ⌋

A   because they're ↑they're↑ not on /ði::/ (.) the public
high:way

In this case we can see that the speaker produces the contribution as a response to someone else's initiation and it is mainly because of this that the whole turn can be heard as a distinct contribution. We know that the speaker produces it to be heard as a response because it is designed to show that it is. So the turn begins with two components that explicitly link it back to the immediately prior turn, i.e. *well* and *yeah*, and continues with an **ellipsed** gramatical form. The ellipsed grammatical form is *it is*. To say that it is ellipsed is to say that a part of the structure is permitted not to occur because that part of the structure can be understood from the context. And the relevant part of the context is speaker B's *actually legal on a car park* which is a part of speaker B's immediately prior turn. This method of achieving cohesion across speaking turns is known as **ellipsis**.

In both cases the contributions are made through turns that involve considerable extension through Same Activity Addition (SAA).

(iv) *Extended turn structure*

To illustrate how an extended turn can be structured I shall examine a turn produced by speaker B, in which she describes a particular episode drawn from her own experience of learning to drive.

Fragment 4

```
B   I think my father would agree with you +
    ↑I remember↑ when I was learning to dri::ve ↑he↑ was on
    this same idea +
    [ of   ] balancing the clutch +
A   [ ye:s ]
B   [ ˙h˙h ] but I hadn't worked out (.) the niceties of steering +
A   [ yes  ]
B   ˙h and we had a dri::ve that was ↑perhaps↑ (.) ° I don't
    kn-↑I↑ don't know how long it was ° +
    ↑but↑ the i:dea was I would start at the bottom +
    ↑not↑ facing the roa[ d (.) ]
                        [ ye:s  ]
B   and I'd go up the dri::ve +
    ˙h but he hadn't allow:ed for the fact that I might end up
    in the ro:se bed +
    [ (.) which I ] quite genuinely did +
A   [ h˙eh˙eh˙   ]
B   [ (.) ] one day: +
A   [ yes ]
B   [ ° and he was     ] not happy ° +
A   [ mm (.) mm (.)yes ]
A   yes
D   mh˙mh˙mh˙
C   [ O-  ]
    [ ° b ] u::t °
```

I take B's main activity to be the describing of a particular incident in which B was involved at some time in the past. A description of the particular incident is relevant at this point in the conversation because it can be related quite directly to the

content of an earlier contribution from A, namely on the importance of learning to balance the clutch. However, several turns
have intervened between that earlier contribution and this turn
of B's. The relevance, for this conversation, of the particular
incident to be described needs therefore to be explicitly reestab-
lished. B carefully designs her turn to do just this by beginning
the turn with turn constructional units, the express purpose of
which is to establish the relevance of the speaker's current
contribution to what has gone before. This can be seen in the
following fragment:

Fragment 5

```
  B   I think my father would agree with you +
      ↑I remember↑ when I was learning to dri::ve ↑he↑ was on
      this same idea +
      ⎡ of   ⎤balancing the clutch +
  A   ⎣ ye:s ⎦
  B   ˙h˙h but I hadn't worked out (.) the niceties of steering +
```

Here we see that the initial turn constructional units are produced to show whose speaking turn the speaking turn that it
initiates is to be related to, what aspect of that speaking turn it is
to be related to, and just how it is to be heard as related. So the
speaking turn it is to be related to is the turn produced by the
participant referred to as *you*; the relevant aspect of that speaking turn is any matter contained within it that can be regarded as
an opinion with which one might *agree*; and it is to be heard as
related through the device of some information regarding *my
father*.

Having thus established the relevance of what is to be said in
this speaking turn for this conversation B then goes on to
provide a narrative account of one particular experience drawn
from the several she could no doubt have recounted as having to
do with her own learning to drive. The narrative account is
delivered through a series of turn constructional units. The
significant event described in this account would seem to be the
driving of the car by B into a rose bed. The significant matter,
therefore, is not the balancing of clutches nor the father's opinion on this matter. Nevertheless, we find that one of the final
turn constructional units reinvokes the significance of the father

as the important point of contact with the turn this turn of B's is
designed to relate to.

    B ° and he was <u>not</u> happy °

So what is introduced as an item whose apparent purpose is
to show some sort of agreement with A's opinion about the
importance of *balancing the clutch* turns out to be used as an
occasion for telling a personal story. But the speaker carefully
builds the turn so that it can be treated as a single relevant
contribution.

(v) *Turn competition*

The most obvious evidence of competition for an opportunity to
speak is the occurrence of overlapping talk. However, it is not
the case that overlapping talk always indicates competition for
the speaker role. The following are some of the possibilities when
competition for a turn is not at issue:

(a)   a recipient's minimal response, perhaps displaying continued acceptance of recipient role, can occur just before the
predictable completion of an activity in the course of an
extended turn:

Fragment 6

  B ↑not↑ facing the road [(.)]
  D   [ye:s]

(b)   a recipient's minimal response, perhaps displaying continued acceptance of recipient role, can occur precisely with,
or just subsequent to, the onset of an extended turn addition:

Fragment 7

  B [and] I'd go up the dri:ve
  D [mm]

(c)   a recipient can say what is predictable as a possible completion of a current speaker's activity in overlap with the
speaker's actual completion, perhaps to display close attention and support:

114

Fragment 8

```
A  ⌈ and ⌉ I've known people get a:ll four:: wrong::
B  ⌊ ye::s ⌋
A  ⌈ and still be passed ⌉
B  ⌊ and still pass     ⌋
```

In none of these cases is there any attempt to take over the speaker role from any other speaker through the use of overlapping talk. Turn competition proper occurs only when this is the case. The following are some of the possibilities.

(d) a recipient initiates a turn when a completion of the current speaker's activity is neither imminent nor predictable:

Fragment 9

```
A  so that people ⌈ are  ⌉ (.) could be ⌈ care::ful   ⌉⌈ when ⌉
B                 ⌊ they ⌋ (.)           ⌊ ↑ they ↑ do ⌋⌊      ⌋
D                                                       ⌊ yes  ⌋
A  ⌈ they've ⌉
B  ⌊ ye::s   ⌋ ↑they do↑ that in France:
A  you have to keep your L plates on or something like that
   for a- ⌈ ↑another↑ ⌉ couple of ⌈ months ⌉ so that er
B         ⌊ mm        ⌋            ⌊ mm     ⌋
A  ⌈ (.) there is ⌉ some warning
B  ⌊ in Fran-     ⌋
```

(e) two or more recipients each initiate a turn at a possible completion point of the current speaker's activity:

Fragment 10

```
A  ↑which↑ I think is ⌈ the most basic skill ⌉ you nee:d
B                     ⌊ h•eh•e ↑haha↑        ⌋
B  •h•h•h ⌈↑I↑    ⌉
D         ⌊↑ It's ⌋ quite↑ a distance though i- ↑in↑ to Castle
   Howard isn't it
```

In the case of fragment 9 it is clear that speaker B has knowledge of a specific piece of information that is directly relevant to the contribution speaker D has just completed. However, before speaker B can begin a turn and get a hearing for this piece of information, speaker A begins a turn. Rather than wait for a possible completion point, and perhaps thereby lose the opportunity of making a contribution that can be heard as directly relevant to another speaker's just completed contribution, speaker B attempts to initiate a turn whilst speaker A's current turn is still in progress. In doing so, speaker B uses raised pitch.

In the case of fragment 10, the motivation for the competition for the speaking turn can again be appreciated by considering what is happening just before the overlapping talk occurs. Speaker A is responding to a comment on the length of the driveway of his house. As he is doing this speaker B begins to laugh. The laughter is not produced at a possible completion point and cannot plausibly be related to any particular thing speaker A is saying. The laughter can be seen to be doing two things. Firstly, it can be seen as a display of the fact that what has been said has touched off an amusing memory. Secondly, and additionally, it can be seen as B giving notice that when an opportunity for a speaking turn occurs, B will use the turn to share what is remembered as amusing.

Fragment 11

```
A  ↑well::↑ (.) it's:: 1- ↑long↑ enough:: to be able /tu::/ (.) you
   know (.) practi⌈ se that  ⌉one thing:: ↑which↑ I think is
B              ⌊ •hu•hu•h ⌋

A  ⌈ the most basic skill ⌉you nee:d
B  ⌊ h•eh•e↑ haha↑      ⌋

B  •h•h•h ⌈↑I↑   ⌉
         ⌊↑It's⌋ quite↑ a distance though i- ↑in↑ to Castle
   Howard isn't it
```

So B has a clear motivation to initiate her contribution at the earliest opportunity. As it turns out, and as we saw earlier, B does go on to share the memory as an amusing anecdote. But because the opportunity to do so is delayed, due to D's competitive turn, B has to reestablish its relevance.

D, on the other hand, has a motivation for competing for the turn because he wants to use it to deliver a quip that can work *only* if delivered immediately after A's turn. Castle Howard is a local stately home and so what D's turn is clearly intended to imply is the amusing idea that A lives in such a place. If B gets the turn, then the only cpportunity for the quip will have passed. Hence the need to compete. Again both B and D use markedly raised pitch as they compete for the turn.

(vi) *Control of turn allocation*
When there are just two people participating in a conversation, the issue of who shall speak next after a possible transition point is quite straightforward. Either the current speaker continues or the other participant takes the turn. If there are more than two participants and the current speaker does not elect to continue, then the problem of which one of the other participants has the right to speak arises. In some situations responsibility is vested in a particular individual to decide who shall speak next, e.g. the chairman in the BBC programme *Question Time*, the teacher in the school classroom, the judge in a law court.

However, this cannot be the case in casual conversation, in which there seem to be two possibilities. The current speaker will in some way indicate who is to speak next, and then that person has the right and obligation to do so. If the current speaker does not select a next speaker, then whoever speaks first has the right to the turn.

The current speaker has, in addition to non-verbal means, two verbal ways of indicating who is to speak next. The speaker can make it clear, through the use of the second person pronoun *you* and reference to 'person specific' people and events, just who is to speak next, e.g. *How was the trip to London?* – which of course makes the assumption that just one of the participants in a conversation in which this might be used is actually known to have made a recent trip to London.

Fragment 12
   D   ↑What↑ was the frustration with your <u>wi:fe</u> then

This mode of selection is most often used when speakers wish to select the participant who had the speaker role immediately before themselves.

The second mode of speaker selection is by specific nomination, i.e. through the use of an individual's name:

Fragment 13

```
D  ↑Can I↑ ↑can I↑ jus::t ask you i-i- ↑com↑ing back John
   ⎡ to the  ⎤ act ⎡ ual ⎤ procedure that you u::se when you
A  ⎣ h•mh•m ⎦     ⎣ yes ⎦
D  teach ⎡ some ⎤ body
A        ⎣ yes: ⎦
D  to drive ↑yo-↑ you ↑get↑ ⎡ (.) ⎤ them going up and down
A                            ⎣ •h  ⎦
D  your:: (.) dri::ve
A  well ↑I↑ get them (.) . . .
```

This particular instance of speaker selection involves D selecting
A who was not the immediately prior speaker.

Activity 6.2

(i) Which participant's topic contributions are mostly other-
initiated? What does this suggest about how the role/status
of this participant is perceived by the other participants for
this interaction?

(ii) Which participant is responsible for most of the minimal
acknowledgements (*mm, yes, sure* and the like), and non-
competitive overlaps? What does this suggest about the
role/status this participant adopts for this interaction?

(iii) Which participant is involved in most of the competitive bids
for a speaking turn? What does this suggest about the
participant?

(iv) Which participant produces most of the explicit next-speaker
selections in the course of the conversation? What does this
tell us about the role/status this participant adopts for the
interaction?

7. Patterns in speech activities

7.1 Introduction

In our discussions so far frequent reference has been made to participants' activities performed in the course of spoken verbal interaction. Some of these activities have to do with the management of the talk as talk being produced for verbal interaction. Others have to do with the very point of the interaction itself.

So, for example, when we seek to repair in some way what we or our interactional partners have said – because there has been a grammatical error, a wrong choice of word, a sense that an appropriate level of politeness has not been achieved or the like – then we are engaging in an activity that has to do with the management of the talk as talk being produced for verbal interaction. Similarly when we seek to make a topic contribution in such a way as to display its relevance for the particular conversation and the conversation's particular participants our activity has to do with the management of talk. These activities we can refer to as **talk management activities**.

The other sorts of activity that have figured in our discussions are in a sense more fundamental than these talk management activities. These other activities are really the point of interaction and the talk management activities are in their service. Thus we engage in interaction with others to express our attitudes, feelings and opinions, to seek and give information, to get others to do things with or for us, to enter into and to disengage from commitments etc. When the spoken word is the means for the performance of these activities we can refer to them as **speech activities**.

Activity 7.1

In the following fragment of conversation between a mother and her two-and-a-half-year-old daughter identify what talk management activity and what speech activity you think the participants engage in.

> *C* Want a bic bic
> *M* Par:don
>   (1.5)
> *C* I would <u>like</u> a bic bic
> *M* That's better
> *C* Please

Discussion

If I were asked to summarise what had gone on in this fragment of conversation I would say that the child had asked the mother for something – **made a request** – and that the mother had got the child to change the way in which she originally made the request – **initiated a repair**. Of course, the request could have been successfully completed without any repair having been initiated but there could be no repair without the request. The repair then is in the service of the request. The repair is the talk management activity and the request, as the point of this bit of verbal interaction, is the speech activity.

7.2 Talk management activities

We shall now look in turn at how talk management activities and speech activities might be investigated. To illustrate the investigation of a talk management activity we shall look at just how one such activity is done. We shall look at how a particular group of people seek to repair a particular aspect of someone else's talk. We shall in fact look at how parents get their children to make their requests more polite.

A first thing to notice is that I have used the word *repair* and not the word *correct*. I have done this because we often want to get someone to change the way in which they have said something even though what they have said does not contain any recognisable error. So the word *repair* is meant to capture a wider range of reasons for effecting a change in the way something has been said than can be captured in the word *correct*.

Conversations between parents and young children who are still acquiring language are rather special. They are special in part because there is such a difference between the participants in the skills of language use that they have. But they are special also because of the particular role that parents often see themselves as having with regard to their children's developing language skills. Many parents see it as part of their parenting role to actively teach their children how language should be used and how talk should be organised.

One mechanism that can be used in the teaching process is of course the mechanism of repair. The child says something the parent deems to be in need of repair and then the parent does a relevant repair. We might then hypothesise that when a child asks for something in a manner that does not meet the standards of politeness required by the parent then the parent will repair what the child has said.

But just how do parents accomplish the task of repairing their children's talk? In the following fragment, for example, the child says something which the parent decides is in need of repair and immediately proceeds to do the relevant repair.

    C   What's that (.) what's that
    M   That's erm er that's a bird called an owl
    C   /aeloː/
→   M   An owl not an /ɛlo/

Activity 7.2

Decide which of the following most accurately describes the things done by the mother and child that are relevant to the repair of the child's talk. Give reasons for your choice:

(i)   The child pronounced something incorrectly and the mother corrected her.

(ii) The child said something and the mother pointed out that it was wrong.

(iii) The mother didn't like the child's pronunciation of a word so pointed out that it was wrong and then provided a correct version.

(iv) The child pronounced a word in a way that deviated from the norms of adult usage and the mother decided not to let the pronunciation pass. So, first she provided an adult pronunciation of the word and then drew the child's attention to the incorrectness of her own original version by repeating it.

Discussion

In trying to describe what is going on within a sequence of talk we should restrict ourselves to the evidence our data provides but at the same time be sure that we include in our descriptions *all* there is in our data that could be relevant. To say that the mother didn't like the child's pronunciation would go beyond the available data. It might well be that the mother was actually highly amused by the child's pronunciation. On the other hand to simply say that the mother corrected the child would tell us little of how it was done and there is indeed available in the data evidence of just how the mother set about her task. For example, she both identified what was wrong and provided an alternative version. Furthermore she did these two things in a particular order.

The mother constructs a turn in which she does two things. She identifies what it was about the child's turn that she has decided was in need of repair and she displays for the child how the relevant item should be repaired. The turn thus has two components. A component that displays the relevant repair – *An owl* – and a component that identifies the item in need of repair – *not an /elo/.*

Activity 7.3

Compare the following fragment with the one just considered and decide what the mother does and how she does it.

C   On the te-'h 'h on the 'h telephone
      (2.0)
M   It isn't a telephone it's a (.) tape-recorder

Discussion

In this fragment the mother decides not to let the child's use of
the word *telephone* to pass and so produces a turn with two
components through which she repairs the child's use of *telephone*. In the first component the mother signals what is in need
of repair and in the second component she displays for the child
what should have been used instead. Essentially the same things
are going on here as in the earlier example except that the
ordering of components in the mother's turn differs.

___

The two fragments thus suggest a possible pattern to the
organisation of repairs. The pattern might be set out as follows:

First speaker: Turn containing what next speaker decides to
                   treat as an item in need of repair
Second speaker: Turn component which identifies repairable
                   item

                   +

Turn component which displays alternative

OR

Turn component which displays alternative

                   +

Turn component which identifies repairable
item

So, on the basis of these conversational fragments, we can say
that this pattern of repair can occur when what is taken to be in
need of repair can be identified and what the necessary repair
might be is known.

If asked to formulate a hypothesis on just how parents set
about repairing their children's requests we might now reason as
follows. Parents will seek to repair a child's request if some
expected **marker of politeness** is lacking. This does not mean that
every time a politeness marker is lacking a parent will seek to

have it included – often they will let it pass – merely that the lack of a politeness marker is the necessary trigger for the process. If parents can recognise the absence of a politeness marker then that means that they know what the relevant politeness marker should have been. They are therefore in a position to identify for the child that a marker is lacking and to propose to the child how the lack should be repaired.

A mother who decides that a politeness marker is missing from a child's request might then seek to repair the child's talk using a pattern similar to that used in the case of the pronunciation of the word *owl* and the appropriate choice of word for a tape-recorder – by signalling what, in the mother's view, is in need of repair and by displaying for the child how the request should have been done or **formatted**.

So that we properly understand what is meant by the expression 'marker of politeness' let's first consider some of the ways in which politeness can be shown or **marked** in requests.

Activity 7.4 _____

The following are all possible ways of asking for things. List them in the order most polite to least polite and decide what it is about each way of asking for something that makes it polite.

erm (.) I don't suppose there are (.) any biscuits (.) left are there

I don't suppose there are any biscuits left are there

I want a biscuit

no chance of a biscuit I suppose

I wonder if I could have a biscuit

I erm (.) wonder if (.) I could have a biscuit

give me a biscuit

I was wondering if I could have a biscuit

biscuit please

darling just one of those plain biscuits if you don't mind

Discussion

It is probable that no two people would rank these ways of asking for something in exactly the same order of politeness. Nevertheless there will be a tendency to treat as more polite those ways of asking for something which are more tentative, which soften the request in some way or which minimise it.

So I would rank

I was wondering if I could have a biscuit

as more polite than

I wonder if I could have a biscuit

because the use of the past progressive form *was wondering* makes it more tentative. On the other hand I would rank

I erm (.) wonder if (.) I could have a biscuit

as more polite than either because of the hesitations that clearly signal tentativeness.

Now that we have some sense of how parents can try to repair children's talk and what sorts of things politeness markers can be, let's suggest an initial hypothesis about how parents might set about the repair of children's requests that lack politeness markers:

Hypothesis: When parents seek to repair children's requests that lack politeness markers they will do so by the use of a two-component turn through which they display for the child that a politeness marker is lacking and just what politeness marker is lacking.

Activity 7.5

Examine again the fragment in which the child was making a request and:

(i) decide what, if anything, the mother does that is directly relevant to the activity of repairing the child's request;

(ii) decide what, if anything, the child does that is directly relevant to the repair of her own request.

C   Want a bic bic
M   Par:don
      (1.5)
C   I would <u>like</u> a bic bic
M   That's better
C   Please

Discussion

What certainly does not happen is that the mother immediately displays to the child just what politeness marker is lacking. To this extent the hypothesis is disconfirmed. What the mother in fact does is to produce a turn in which she uses the single word turn constructional unit *pardon*.

The child then, following a pause, produces a turn in which she makes changes to the way in which her request was originally formated. The child shifts from a statement of desire expressed through the word *want* to a statement of preference expressed through the word *like*. The child also introduces the past tense modal auxiliary verb *would*. A statement of preference modified by a past tense auxiliary verb is by convention treated as more polite than a bald statement of desire as a way of formatting a request. They are then to be regarded as markers of politeness. In addition the child finally adds the highly conventionalised marker of politeness *please*.

What is important for us to notice here is that the changes that are made are done entirely by the child. The mother's role here is to say something that somehow gets the child herself to set about making the changes. The mother neither signals that lack of a politeness marker is an issue nor what the necessary but lacking politeness marker might be. And this despite the fact that the mother is clearly concerned with getting the child to provide a missing politeness marker. We know this because the mother goes on to make an evaluative comment on the changes once they have been made. The evaluative comment is done through the turn constructional unit *That's better*.

We should then revise our initial hypothesis and suggest instead that parents, initially at least, simply indicate that there is something amiss without specifying what or how it might be remedied, but signal in a subsequent turn that the repair done is the repair aimed for.

Hypothesis: When parents seek to repair children's requests that lack politeness markers this is done over a four-turn sequence that has the following pattern:

> *Child*:   Request
> *Mother*: Minimal form clarification request
> (*What, Pardon* etc.)
> *Child*:   Modified request to show politeness
> *Mother*: Evaluation of request modification

Activity 7.6

Consider the following parental attempts to get children to repair the requests they have made and decide whether they confirm or disconfirm the hypothesis. Pay particular attention to the apparent exceptions to the hypothesised sequential pattern:

C ↑Put on the ligh::t↑
   (0.9)
M Par:don
   (.)
C Put on the light please
   (.)
M Better

Fragment 2
C ↑M::ore:: chip↑
   (1.3)
C ↑M:ore:: chip↑
   (.)
M ↑Wha::t↑
   (1.5)
C ↑I want↑ more::: chip
M ↑What↑
   (.)
C Want more:: chips =
M ↑More chips what↑
   (.)
C Plea:se
   (.)
M Ye::s I should think so

Fragment 3
C Hey
   (0.7)

Pull up the ro:pe with thi:s dow:n
(0.9)

M ↑I beg your pardon↑
(.)

C Plea:se
(.)

M No: I don't understand what you're saying what do you mean

Let's now consider just what was involved in the mother's getting the child to repair her talk. The mother initiates the repair but does not herself do the repair. We can say that the repair in this case is **other-initiated**, i.e. initiated by someone *other* than the person who produced the item deemed to be in need of repair.

But the repair is actually done as a **self-repair**, i.e. done by the *selfsame* person who produced the repairable item. The repair here then is an **other-initiated self-repair**.

So there are in fact different ways in which repair can be handled as a talk management activity. For example, the person *other* than the person who produced the repairable item can do the repair. In such a case we can say that there has been an **other-initiated other-repair**. This was the case in the fragment where the mother repairs the child's pronunciation of the word *owl*. A further possibility is that the person who produces a repairable item both sets in motion the process of repair and indeed does the repair. In this case we can talk of **self-initiated self-repair**. Following is an example of such a self-initiated self-repair of a request. Here a child uses the repair to defer what she is asking for until some later point in time with the expression *In a minute* and this could be seen as a way of making the original request more polite.

C ↑can my↑ just (.) come
(2.0)

→ Can my (.) in a (.) minute

M Alright

But in the sequence types we are considering the repairs are other-initiated. How are they other-initiated? The repairs are initiated by the mother's use of the expression *Pardon* and the like. On the face of it, *Pardon* should strike us as a somewhat strange expression to use since it would seem, in part at least, to ask for some sort of forgiveness and thereby to imply that the producer of the expression is in some sense at fault.

But what is being signalled here is precisely the opposite. Or at least that is the interpretation put on the use of the expression by the child to whom the *Pardon* is addressed. For the child behaves as if she has been at fault for not having included a politeness marker in her request. Why then should *Pardon* be used and how can it be given the interpretation it is in fact given?

First, let us consider a use of the expression *Pardon* where some sort of fault is indeed being ascribed to herself by the producer of the expression.

C   /kɪs/ goes in (.) into her bucket
M   Par:don
C   /kɪs/ goes into her bucket
M   ↑Chris↑ goes into his bucket
C   Ye:s

Now one of the things that seem to be at issue here is the child's pronunciation of a name. We can tell that there is a quite genuine problem here because the mother eventually asks the child to confirm that what she is hearing should be heard as the name *Chris*. A problem that a listener might have with someone else's pronunciation can arise because of poor articulation or because the listener failed to give full attention to what was being said. If the first case, then the fault is with the speaker; but if the second, then the fault is with the listener. By using *Pardon* here the listener is signalling to the original speaker that a problem has arisen because of her own inattention and not because of the speaker's articulation. It doesn't really matter whether the mother really believed that the problem was due to her own inattention. What matters is that this is what she wants to signal and she can do this with the expression *Pardon*.

I have stressed that the problem of hearing/understanding is genuine here in order to contrast it with the case of the requests that we have been considering. In the case of the requests it was clear that the mother knew what and how repair should be done. There was no question of checking with the child for confirmation of what repair should be done. This issue of genuine versus non-genuine problems of hearing/understanding can lead to actual misunderstandings as is illustrated in the following fragment:

C   Hey
(0.7)
Pull up the ro:pe with thi:s dow:n
(0.9)
M   ↑I beg your pardon↑
(.)
Plea:se
(.)
M   No: I don't understand what you're saying what doyou mean

So we have seen that the expression used by the mother to initiate a repair to the child's request is an expression that can be used to signal a problem of hearing/understanding. Furthermore it can be used to signal that the problem is in some way the fault of the person using the expression.

The following fragments are examples of the expression's use where a parent is trying to get a child to supply politeness markers for requests:

C   Want a bic bic
M   Par:don
(1.5)
C   I would <u>like</u> a bic bic
M   That's better
C   Please

C   ↑Put on the li::ght↑
(0.9)
M   Par:don
(.)
C   Put on the light please
M   Better

In both of these cases the child interprets the mother's *Pardon* as initiating a repair with respect to the politeness of the original request. And in both cases the mother's evaluative comment on the completed repair shows that the fault is perceived as a fault of the child's and not of the mother's. How then does the expression come to be used in order to get a child to supply a missing politeness marker whose lack is manifestly perceived as the fault of the child and not of the person using the expression?

I don't think that the answer to this can lie in an inspection of what is going on in people's minds when they initiate the repair of requests in this way. The practice is so general as almost certainly to be automatic. But what we can say is that, whether intended or not, this way of repairing requests is an excellent way of raising a young child's awareness of how they use language and of how they are expected to use language. This is because the use of *Pardon* and the like puts the responsibility of repair squarely on the shoulders of the child. It is for the child to decide what, if anything, is wrong and it is for the child to decide how it should be put right. And in being put in a position to have to make these decisions the child is led into a sense of personal responsibility for achieving appropriate levels of politeness in her dealings with others. Perhaps this is just one expression of the teaching role that parents more or less subconsciously adopt in their dealings with young children.

The investigation of talk management activities should then reveal what tasks are performed in the accomplishment of the activity, how turns and sequences of turns are designed through which the tasks are performed, and what is achieved by the use of one sort of pattern or structure rather than another. In brief, we should set ourselves the following questions in approaching the investigation of talk management activities:

  (i) What gets done?
 (ii) What are the design details of the speaking turns that do whatever gets done?
(iii) Who does what?
 (iv) In what order do the participants do the things they do?
  (v) What difference does a difference in turn design, participant involvement or sequence of turns make?

7.3 Speech activities

Let us now turn to the investigation of speech activities. There are three respects in which these activities, which we can refer to as **speech activities**, are fundamental to the organisation of verbal interaction.

Firstly, almost anything we say will have some purpose behind it and the activities done in speaking turns are a means to achieving those purposes. Secondly, whatever speech activity we use, a speaking turn to perform that activity will almost certainly place restrictions on what sort of speech activity a next speaker may perform. And thirdly, turn-taking in spoken verbal interaction depends on participants' ability to recognise those places in someone's talk where the activity being performed might be properly considered to be complete.

We shall begin our discussion of how to approach the investigation of speech activities by considering how we might describe an incident in a soccer match.

Activity 7.7

Discuss the meanings of the following terms as they might be used in the description of an incident in a soccer match: *kick, pass, cross, shoot.*

Discussion

If we say of someone that they have *kicked* a ball we say no more than that they have moved their leg in such a way as to bring their foot into contact with the ball so that the ball was made to move. Now this might well be a factually correct description of a player's action but it would not be a particularly informative description given that what is being described is an action performed in the context of a soccer match. If, on the other hand, we had said that the player in question had *passed* the ball then this would be much more informative, at least to those familiar with the game of soccer.

To say that someone has *passed* the ball in a game of soccer is to say that the player has not only *kicked* the ball but that in addition the ball has been *kicked* with a very specific purpose – namely, to have the ball come under the control of a player on the same side as the player kicking the ball. This is not to imply that two separate things are going on at the same time but rather to suggest that what you see can be described from two points of view. The player's action can either be described as a bodily movement or as an action performed specifically in the context of a game of soccer. The context of the game of soccer establishes that there are 'sides' or 'teams' made up of numbers of players; that, unlike in tennis, players on the same side are allowed to exchange control of the ball; and that exchange of the ball is a routine activity performed in order to further the overall aims of the teams within the game.

Furthermore, to say that someone has *passed* the ball is to treat what has happened not as an isolated act but as a span of activity with component parts and reciprocating activity on the part of some other party. So passing a ball requires communicating to some other party that that is what you are about to do; the potential receiver must signal their availability to receive the pass; some assessment must be made of how and where it would be best for the receiver to receive the ball etc.

Similarly, if one were to say that someone had *crossed* a ball then this description would certainly indicate that the physical action of kicking had occurred but would also indicate that a span of activity with a particular purpose, possibly made up of component elements, had occurred. To understand that purpose we would need to be familiar with the layout of a soccer pitch, direction of play etc. And to describe an action as *shooting* in the context of a game of soccer is to indicate that not only has someone kicked a ball but that in addition the ball has been kicked with a very specific purpose in mind – namely, to make the ball pass between the goal posts. Again, this purpose makes sense only if we are familiar with the rules and practices of soccer.

In short, to say that someone has *passed* a ball, *crossed* a ball, or *shot* in a game of soccer is to say that in kicking the ball they have done so with particular purposes and those purposes make sense and can be described only by reference to the rules and practices of the game of soccer. It is important to note that whilst players can, for example, pass balls in other games such as rugby the different rules and practices of these games change the nature of *passing* with respect to either purpose or method of performance.

The rules of games can be highly formalised and more or less rigid, as with soccer, tennis, chess, etc., or they can be informal and *ad hoc* rules created just for the particular game, participants and circumstances, as when we invent games of tag, ball-passing routines on the beach etc. Similarly the rules of interaction can be highly formalised as in certain ritualised ceremonies like marriages, routine occasions like business meetings, job interviews, doctor/patient consultations etc., or rather looser frameworks within which we do things like ask friends to do us favours, make arrangements to go out, tell each other good or bad news etc. This similarity has led some, most notably the philosopher Wittgenstein, to refer to the different sorts of **language game** that we engage in when we interact with others.

So, as we shall see, speech activities are in some ways like the activities performed in the course of games. They involve more than just the observable physical behaviour, they involve purposes that can only be understood by reference to some wider context of rules and practices. And just as a pass in football can be the first part of a one–two move that is designed to lead to a shot at goal – and its significance therefore only be interpretable in the light of this – so in verbal interaction we shall see too that speech activities can be organised as sequences with the interpretation of individual activities being highly dependent on an activity's sequential position.

When someone performs an activity in the course of a game of soccer it's rarely the case that they explicitly signal just what activity it is that they are performing. Other players and observers of the game must work out for themselves an interpretation of each individual action or series of actions. It's then only in reports of incidents that activities are actually named. Much the same applies in the case of our talk. It's true we do sometimes find ourselves saying things like:

> I'd like to ask you a favour
> Just one more question, if you don't mind
> Clarify that for me, will you
> I agree
> Must tell you this joke I just heard
> I really must complain about the way you've treated us
> Promise I'll be there
> Please

All of these expressions we can imagine being used to signal that our purpose at the particular point in interaction is the doing of an activity of a particular kind. But it's also the case that activities are done and recognised without any explicit signalling of this kind. Explicit reference to the various activities that get done in speaking turns is most likely in subsequent reports of interaction. But the reports, of course, are produced as activities in their own right in later conversations. It's in such reports that we say things like:

He **promised** me he'd come
He **invited** me round
She **agreed** with what I was saying
She was full of **quips**
He **complained** to me about it
She **criticised** the whole thing
I got the usual **request** for more money
She **told** me this **horrific story** about the holiday
I had to **acknowledge** she had a good point
She was very **complimentary** about my essay
I **challenged** his position on that

But it's just as likely that in subsequent reports of activities done in talk we would use expressions like:

She **says**, 'You didn't.' And I **goes**, 'I did.' So she says 'Get lost!'
I just went, 'Charming!' and walked off.

The use of expressions such as *say* and *go* to report speech is equivalent to the use of *kick* in reports of a soccer match. They report the directly observable behaviour but do not take account of the purposes that could be the basis for interpreting the behaviour.

Activity 7.8

In pairs tell each other about some recent conversation you have had. An observer should note down how each of you reports what the participants in the reported conversation were doing with the words they were using. For example, it might be reported that someone promised to do something, or that someone asked for something, or that someone criticised someone for having done something etc. Use the observer's notes to remind you of what was reported as happening and then quiz each other about the basis used for having said that someone had made a promise, criticised etc.

Discussion

You will have probably found this a very difficult activity. It is most unusual to have to account for our claims about what has gone on in a conversation. Not only is it unusual, it is also usually rather annoying for the person being quizzed on such matters – at least this has been my experience when I have tried to pin people down in this way. One group of people who do do this sort of thing – albeit in a speculative picture-building sort of way – are writers. The following is an excellent example providing lots of pointers to possible hypotheses.

This extract from Kazuo Ishiguro's novel *The Remains of the Day* is highly suggestive of what might be involved in the recognition and performance of speech activities. Stevens, an ageing butler, has recently entered into service with an American who it seems to Stevens likes to engage in 'banter' in conversation. This sort of behaviour is new to Stevens who is more used to service with the reserved and rather more aloof members of the English aristocracy. Nevertheless, Stevens considers it his professional duty to behave appropriately in the face of another's banter. In other words he sets himself the task of performing a speech activity of the appropriate kind as a response to his employer's banter. Ishiguru's account of Stevens's attempt at an appropriate response is suggestive of what might be involved in the performance and recognition of a speech activity.

'I suppose it wasn't you making that crowing noise this morning, Stevens?'

My employer was referring, I realized, to a pair of gypsies gathering unwanted iron who had passed by earlier making their customary calls. As it happened, I had that same morning been giving thought to the dilemma of whether or not I was expected to reciprocate my employer's bantering, and had been seriously worried at how he might be viewing my repeated failure to respond to such openings. I therefore set about thinking of some witty reply; some statement which would still be safely inoffensive in the event of my having misjudged the situation. After a moment or two, I said:

'More like swallows than crows, I would have said, sir. From the migratory aspect.' And I followed this with a suitably modest smile to indicate without ambiguity that I had made a witticism, since I did not wish Mr Farraday to restrain any spontaneous mirth he felt out of a misplaced respectfulness.

Mr Farraday, however, simply looked up at me and said: 'I beg your pardon, Stevens?'

Only then did it occur to me that, of course, my witticism would not be easily appreciated by someone who was not aware that it was gypsies who had passed by. I could not see, then, how I might press on with this bantering; in fact, I decided it best to call a halt to the matter and, pretending to remember something I had urgently to attend to, excused myself, leaving my employer looking rather bemused.

> (Kazuo Ishiguro, *The Remains of the Day*
> (Faber & Faber, 1989) pp. 16–17)

In this extract several matters with potential relevance for the performance and recognition of speech activities are touched upon. There is the suggestion that the interpretation of some piece of language behaviour is ultimately dependent on the context in which the behaviour is embedded – just as the interpretation of bodily movements can depend on the games in which they occur, so too can the interpretation of utterances depend on the 'language games' of which they are a part. In this case the language game of 'bantering' is assumed.

Stevens raises the question of whether a witticism really is appropriate and suggests that the status of his activity should be submerged in the design of his turn to take account of this uncertainty:

'... some statement which would still be safely inoffensive in the event of my having misjudged the situation.'

So if, for example, Mr Farraday's utterance was a serious request for information with no attendant basis for its being interpreted as having a bantering purpose then a witticism would not have been an expected response. Stevens's problem is then to design an utterance which could be interpreted as humorous but at the same time could be claimed, if challenged perhaps, to have been intended to be interpreted as an appropriate response to a serious question from a superior to a subordinate.

The problem is addressed by Stevens with an utterance design that is formal in choice of vocabulary and grammar but which is followed by a display of its humorous status by the device of a smile.

'I followed this with a suitably modest smile'

What then goes wrong? It would seem that in the design of his utterance Stevens overestimates Mr Farraday's knowledge of the particular context in which Stevens's remark is to be understood:

'my witticism would not be easily appreciated by somone who was not aware that it was gypsies who had passed by'

The connection between gypsies and itinerant swallows is lost and hence the connection with crows which is the basis of the intended witticism.

A further possible source of confusion might be timing. Stevens makes reference to the timing of the speaking turn in which he attempts his quip. He says that it is delivered a moment or two after the utterance that is its trigger or which **occasioned** it. It might well be the case that quips are not the sort of activity whose delivery can be delayed in this way.

These observations suggest that the performance and recognition of a speech activity can depend on:

(i)   the linguistic and non-linguistic context of its performance – where the speaking turn in which the activity is being done occurs relative to other speaking turns, where the interaction is taking place, the overall purposes of the interaction, who is talking to whom and participants' relative states of knowledge;

(ii) utterance design features with respect to vocabulary, grammar, non-verbal behaviours, timing etc.

In our discussion of talk management activities we used instances of talk in which one of the participants was making a request as our data. In our discussion we simply assumed that everyone could recognise a request without any discussion of how in fact they might be recognised in the course of interaction. As a first illustration of how to set about the investigation of a speech activity we shall use the activity of requesting.

Activity 7.9

When we make requests we ask other people to do things for us or to give us things. The following are examples of the sorts of things we might ask for:

Salt at the dinner table
A lift to school
A classmate's notes
£300 for a school field trip
£300 for a school ski trip
A sandwich, yoghurt and Coke at the lunch counter
A telephone number from Directory Enquiries

Role-play the making of these requests with an observer who should note down differences in the way the requests are made. Discuss whether the differences have to do with the circumstances in which the request is made, the participants involved or with the nature of the request itself.

Discussion

A number of differences should have been apparent. Sometimes, for example, the request would have been made without any preamble as almost certainly will have been the case with asking for salt at the dinner table. Some of the requests will have been done with a lot of politeness-marking whilst others will have been relatively free of such marking. It's likely that asking for things at the lunch counter would fall into this latter category. Built into the way some of the things were asked for will have been all manner of explanations and justifications. Such would no doubt have been the case where large sums of money would be involved. Even where politeness was an issue it is likely that the forms chosen to mark politeness will have differed according, for example, to the relationship between the participants involved.

Following are transcriptions of three conversational fragments in which a wife asks her husband to do something for her.

Request 1 – a transcription

(*Husband and wife are preparing a meal for visiting friends. The husband has just taken a telephone call from the friends.*)

Husband	Said they'd be here for eight
	(0.5)
Wife	OK
	(0.5)
	Should be just about ↑ready↑ (.) I think
Husband	Goo::d
	(0.5)
Wife	↑Do you want /tuː/↑ erm <u>emp</u>ty the dishwasher while ↑I↑ set the table
Husband	Yeah alright

Request 2 – a transcription

(*Husband and wife are about to go out and the husband has just made for the door of the room in which they have been sitting to get his coat etc.*)

Wife	Are you going ↑upstairs↑
Husband	Yeàh
Wife	Will you fetch my trainers down for me
Husband	Yeah alright
Wife	Thanks

Request 3 – a transcription

(*Husband and wife are in the kitchen of their home having both separately just arrived home from work. The husband is making a cup of tea. The children referred to in the conversation are the children of the wife's first marriage and live with her former husband.*)

Husband	↑Sorry↑
Wife	Going to fetch the <u>chil</u>dren this weekend I just been talking to <u>Rach</u>el
Husband	Oh yeah

Wife	And erm ↑thing is↑ she finishes ear::ly on Fri::day and Stuart's got (.) there's a training day at school as well so Stuart's off (.) so:: (.) they could come up earlier (0.5) ⌈ than ⌉ y'know than the usual ti::me
Husband	⌊ mmyeah ⌋
	(0.5)
Wife	if we can kind of sort out picking them ↑u::p↑ (0.5) what (.) ⌈ ↑what you doing↑ ⌉ on Friday
Husband	⌊ Can't they get ⌋
	(1.0)
	What am ↑I↑ doing (.) ⌈ ↑ern↑ ⌉ let's think (2.0) ˙h
	⌊ Yeah ⌋
	↑er↑ h˙h˙h˙ (1.5) ↑pretty busy actually↑ ⌈ (0.5) ⌉
Wife	⌊ Are you ⌋
Husband	°thinking about it° ↑yeah↑
Wife	Well I mean ↑I↑ can't (.) I mean ↑ob↑ viously I can't get away (.) I mean I won't be back here till twenty past fi::ve so so like I won't be down there till (.) half past <u>six</u>
Husband	mm
Wife	And then- (0.5) if there's ↑any way↑ that you could (.) finish early I mean do you think you'd be able to ↑fetch↑ them
Husband	Erm::
Wife	It's::- ↑if↑ I c- could go on the train so you could have the car::
Husband	mmyeah
	(1.0)
	Mean I'd (.) <u>like</u> /tu::/ (.) but I can't (.) see how I can get out of erm (0.5) all these (.) <u>damn</u> meetings I've got organised (.) ↑erm↑ (1.5) can:: you er (2.0) give me till tomorrow (.) and I'll see what arrangements I can make
Wife	Yeah (.) OK then

Activity 7.10 _____

For each transcription:

(i) identify the speaking turn in which the wife actually asks for something;

(ii) identify any speaking turn that could be interpreted as indicating that the speaker is about to ask for something;

(iii) describe in detail what it is about the words and/or grammar or paralinguistic features, e.g. stress, rhythm etc. of the relevant turns that makes it likely that the speaker of the turn is asking for something or is about to ask for something;

(iv) describe in detail what it is about the context in which the turns are produced that makes it likely that the speaker of the turn is asking for something or is about to ask for something.

Discussion

Request 1

(i) In this case the turn in which the wife actually asks for something is:

→ *Wife* ↑Do you want /tuː/↑ erm <u>emp</u>ty the dishwasher while ↑I↑ set the table

(ii) In this case there does not seem to be any other turn that is interpretable as indicating that something is about to be asked for.

(iii) In the turn the wife makes reference to a possible future action that the husband could perform:

empty the dishwasher

The wife also raises the issue of the husband's desires in relation to the performance of this future action through the interrogative form:

do you want

The wife also refers to a future action of her own which in fact will be performed at the same time as the possible future action of her husband:

while I set the table

The raised pitch on the pronoun *I* in her reference to her own possible future action highlights the fact that this will be an action which she herself will be performing.

So the turn in which something is asked for can be recognised as doing this, at least in part, because it makes reference to the husband's desires regarding the performance of a possible future action whilst highlighting the contemporaneous performance by the wife of a possible future action.

(iv) The two participants are engaged in the performance of a joint activity i.e. dinner preparation for visiting guests. Any utterance will in such a context be monitored to see if it can be interpreted as furthering the performance of the joint activity. One way of furthering joint activity is through getting others to do things that are coordinated with the overall goal of the activity. We get people to do things by making requests.

Request 2

(i) In this case the turn in which the wife actually asks for something is:

Will you fetch my trainers down for me

(ii) One question that is always at the back of our minds as we hear the speaking turns of others is 'Why did they say that in that way now?'. This question is a useful one to apply when approaching the analysis of other people's conversations. If we apply it to the turn:

Are you going upstairs

then a reasonable assumption, given the circumstances in which the turn is produced, might be that the speaker has some action in mind that can be performed by an individual who is indeed going upstairs.

(iii) The turn which asks for something is formatted as an interrogative. Interrogatives are most often used to ask questions. In this case the question asked is a question about the husband's willingness to do something:

Will you fetch... trainers...

for the benefit of the wife:

my... for me

The turn that might be taken as a signal that something is about to be asked for is also formatted as an interrogative. In this case the question asked through the interrogative is a question about the immediate future actions of the recipient of the question, i.e. the husband.

Are you going upstairs

(iv) The question about the immediate future actions of the husband is produced just as the husband is making for the door of the room in which he has been sitting with his wife. The circumstances in which the question is asked are circumstances in which both he and his wife know that he is about to get ready to go out. Getting ready to go out is also a relevant activity for the wife at this point. Because it is known to both of them that he is about to get ready to go out then the husband's going upstairs is not likely to be the subject of idle enquiry on the part of the wife. His going upstairs, rather than, say, into the garden, is likely to be a highly predictable matter. So in asking the question the wife is likely to have been motivated by some other concern than simply what sort of activity her husband's standing up is the beginning of. Given that the husband is himself likely to be going upstairs in order to do something relevant to their imminent departure then a reasonable interpretation of the wife's question is that there is something to be done upstairs that would also have relevance to her with regard to that imminent departure. All of this could make the question hearable as a signal that something is about to be asked for. Questions of this sort have been referred to as **pre-sequences** because they prefigure something that is to be done in a subsequent turn.

The question about the husband's willingness to perform an action for the benefit of the wife is interpretable as a request largely because of the same features of context that made the earlier question hearable as a pre-sequence to the activity of asking for something.

Request 3

(i) In this case the wife asks for something through a component of a speaking turn:

do you think you'd be able to fetch them

(ii)   A quite clear indication that the wife is about to ask for something is:

what you doing on Friday

which is also produced as a component of a speaking turn in which other things are accomplished.

(iii)   In this case the pre-sequence is an interrogative which is used to ask a question about the husband's activities on the day already specified as the day on which the children are to be collected. We should also note that other components of this turn have to do with the presentation of a problem in relation to the children. The children could be picked up earlier than usual and it is restrictions on taking up this opportunity that is the problem:

if we can sort out picking them up

Furthermore, the presentation of the problem is marked by a good deal of hesitation and hedging:

Wife	And erm ↑thing is↑ she finishes ear::ly on Fri::day and Stuart's got (.) there's training day at school as well so Stuart's off (.) so:: (.) they could come up earlier (0.5) ⌈ than ⌉ y'know than the
Husband	⌊ mmyeah ⌋
Wife	usual ti::me (0.5) if we can kind of sort out picking them ↑u::p↑ (0.5) what (.)

The turn component through which the wife actually asks for something is also an interrogative which is used to ask a question about the husband's assessment

do you think

of his ability to carry out some future action:

you'd be able to fetch them

This turn component is surrounded by other components which either show how she cannot do what is being asked for or show how what is being asked for could be made possible and so granted:

> I can't get away
> I won't be back here till twenty past five so like I won't be down there till half past six
> if there's any way you could finish early
> I could go on the train so you could have the car

And again these turn components are marked by a good deal of hesitation and hedging.

(iv) The crucial aspect of context for identifying the pre-sequence here is the problem presentation by the wife. We should note that the wife refers to the task that both she and her husband are faced with in having to 'sort something out'.

It is likely that by the time the wife gets to the point of actually delivering her pre-sequence the husband is aware that he is to be asked to do something. Evidence for this is that he says in overlap with the wife's pre-sequence:

> Can't they get-

which would seem to be projecting something like *Can't they get the train*. And this, of course, would be a way of forestalling the wife's progress towards actually asking him to fetch the children.

If we compare the way in which the activity of requesting is done in these three cases we can see that in the first case there is no pre-sequence and the request is formatted so as almost to assume compliance. This is presumably the case because of the nature of the request and because of the expectations the participants might have of each other in this particular situation.

In the second case there is some likelihood of a sense of imposition on the husband if it turns out to be the case that he is not going upstairs as part of his preparations to go out. Here then we do have a pre-sequence that checks out what, if it were the case, would minimise any sense of imposition.

The final request is clearly the most delicate to handle since it turns out that it actually does constitute a considerable imposition on the husband. The request does not come out of the blue but is gradually approached by the wife. During this gradual approach it becomes clear what the wife is moving towards and one option open to the husband would, of course, have been for him to make an offer to try and arrange things so that he could fetch the children. He does not do this but the pattern followed by the wife in making this last request can be seen as providing opportunities for just this to happen.

The formatting and interpretation of requesting would thus seem to depend on the nature of what is being asked for, the participants involved and the circumstances surrounding the making of the request.

Requests, as with most activities in conversation, are things that the makers of requests expect responses to. Sometimes we respond to requests by granting them and sometimes we respond to them by not granting them. If we examine what happens in response to the three requests that are under investigation here we can see that the first two requests are granted whilst the third is not.

Activity 7.11 _____

Compare the formats of the husband's responses to the first two requests with his response to the third.

Discussion

In the first two cases the husband makes clear straight away and without any room for doubt that he will do what is being asked of him. In the third request his response behaviour is quite different. He delays his response in various ways. He displays regret for not being in a position to do what is being asked of him. He provides an account for why he can't do what is being asked of him. And he defers any final response to some later time.

Activity 7.12 _____

Identify the turn components through which the husband:

  (i)   delays;
 (ii) displays regret;
(iii) provides an account;
(iv) defers.

  (i) → *Husband* (1.0)
      →   What am ↑I↑ doing
      →   (.)

→		↑erm↑ let's think	
→		(2.0)	
→		•h ↑er↑ h•h•h•	
→		(1.5)	
(ii)	→	*Husband*	Mean I'd (.) <u>like</u> /tu::/
(iii)	→	*Husband*	I can't (.) see how I can get out of erm (0.5)
			all these (.) <u>damn</u> meetings I've got organised
(iv)	→	*Husband*	can:: you er (2.0) give me till tomorrow (.)
			and I'll see what arrangements I can make

Now it might end up that the husband does fetch the children. It might be the case that though he really wants to help he simply can't. Or it might be the case that he has no intention at all of rearranging things. In analysing this piece of interaction we shouldn't take account of the husband's presumed psychological states. All we can say is that the husband has chosen one way of responding to a request rather than another. He has chosen not to grant the request. But in choosing not to grant the request he has engaged in the activity of not granting the request in a particular way. The not granting of the request has had particular attention drawn to it in the the way that the husband has formatted his response. The husband has in fact made the response a rather complicated affair with its delays, displays of regret, accounts and deferrals. This complexity has the effect of displaying the activity as something that all else being equal would be avoided.

When an activity is formatted so as to have this complexity we can say that the activity is formatted to display that it is an activity that has a **dispreferred** status. Without this complexity the format of an activity is said to display its **preferred** status. So for all activities that expect some one from a set of particular activities in response then those activities will be so formatted as to show there preferred or dispreferred status.

Activity 7.13

Suggest preferred and dispreferred formats for responses to the following activities:

A compliment
A criticism of a third party
An invitation
An enquiry about your health

Following is a transcription of a fragment of talk that occurs at the beginning of a consultation between a doctor and his patient. There is some confusion over just how a particular turn should be interpreted. Investigation of this confusion and how it might have arisen should help us further clarify what can be involved in the performance and recognition of speech activities.

Doctor/patient consultation – a transcription

D ↑Come in↑
 (2.0)
P ↑Hello↑
 (1.5)
 I've just come for a repeat (.) prescription
 (.)
D Right
P I'm ↑I'm↑ a temporary resident =
D = Yes:: (.) ⌈ sure ⌉ going h.h. back tonight and er
P ⌊ ↑I'm↑ ⌋
 ⌈ (.) ⌉ as usual
D ⌊ mm ⌋
P ↑chaos↑ as usual I've run out ↑just↑ when I need them
 ↑heheheh↑
→ *D* So what are you taking
→ *P* I'm taking politics
 (1.0)
D No I mean pills
P Oh

Activity 7.14

The following are both imaginable responses to the question: So what are you taking

Just some shorts and tee shirts.
The train.

Each assumes a different interpretation of the question. Devise scenarios for each of the imaginable responses.

Discussion

Whichever response is focused on the relevant scenario must take account of the fact that the question that precedes the response is itself embedded within some sequence. It is not, in other words, a question out of the blue. This is indicated through the use of the item *So* which explicitly indicates that the question is to be heard as related to something that is understood from the foregoing linguistic or non-linguistic context.

In the case of the response referring to clothes I could imagine it being said by a son or daughter to a parent as they prepare to leave on an inter-rail holiday. Or I could imagine it being said by a refugee to a supervisor of clothes distribution in a refugee camp. In the case of the refugee one might expect the question and response to occur towards the end of the interaction, for example, following the rummaging through of a bin of clothes.

In the case of the response referring to the train one could imagine this in the course of casual conversation between friends about holiday arrangements or it could figure in the course of an interaction where directions are being given, in which case the question would have been understood as preliminary to some quite specific further detailing of directions, i.e. details relevant to someone arriving by train.

What these outlines of the different scenarios suggest is that the interpretation of an utterance depends on the type of interaction it occurs in, where it occurs in the interaction, who is talking to whom and what the parties to the interaction know about each other, the interaction and its context.

These observations can now be brought to bear on the actual confusion that arises in the doctor/patient consultation.

Activity 7.15

Suggest what it might be about the type of interaction, where it occurs in the interaction, whose speaking turn it is, and what the participants might be presumed to know about each other that

gives rise to the response that turns out to be based on a misinterpretation:

I'm taking politics

Discussion

As was pointed out earlier this response is a response to a
question. It is recognisable as a question because of its grammar.
It is interrogative in form. The question was designed to be heard
as following from something known in common because of the
linguistic or non-linguistic context. The doctor's *So* which introduces the interrogative format is the crucial design feature here.
A first thing a recipient of such a question might do is to search
for something that is indeed known in common and on which the
question might therefore be focusing. What is known in common
is that both participants are in a doctor/patient consultation.
Furthermore, they are in the earlier stages of the consultation
where it is usual to exchange information of a more socially
bonding kind, often referred to as **phatic communication**, before
moving on to exchanges of a more specifically professional kind.
In the speaking turn that immediately precedes the question the
patient has been accounting for her visit at this particular point
in time rather than use the turn to make clear her main interactional purpose which is to make a request for a specific prescription item. And crucially we should note that her account is so
formulated as to incorporate particular assumptions about what
the doctor knows about her. We could say that her turn has a
quite particular **recipient design** in that it refers to student-related
activities and routines without specifying in so many words her
student status. The account thus embdies an assumption that her
student status is known to the doctor.

temporary resident
going back tonight

The turn that precedes the doctor's question is thus designed
with the assumption that her student status is known to the
doctor. So it is easy to see how the doctor's immediately following question can be interpreted as invoking her student status.
She thinks the question is of the phatic non-professional kind.
She thinks the doctor knows she's a student. The question is

designed to show a connection with her turn that implied but did not state her student status. That student status could therefore be an obvious focus of general social chat as a preliminary to the more professional talk to follow.

So the misinterpretation of what precise activity was being performed in the doctor's turn clearly points up what can be involved in successful recognition and performance of speech activities. How an activity should be performed and how it will be interpreted depends on how it is formulated, where it occurs in the sequence of talk, and participants' perceptions of the situation, each other and the purposes of the interaction.

Questions and requests are relatively easy to identify in an unfolding interaction. But most of the things we do in interaction are perhaps not quite so easy to identify and characterise. So let's now consider another activity as it occurs in the course of a police interrogation of a suspect. In this case just what activity is being performed is rather less obvious than in the previous examples. The police know that the suspect has made a telephone call on the morning of the interrogation to the victim of the alleged crime.

Police interrogation – a transcription (adapted)

D Why did you ring him this morning
S This morning (.) because I was very annoyed at the
   situation with (.) when another one of your police
   officers came and started banging on the door last night
   (3.0)
   the same situation
   (.)
→ D A police officer came to your door last night
S I had people ⌈ banging ⌉
D   ⌊ Was this ⌋ a uniformed officer
   (0.5)
S No idea
D So how would you know that it was a police officer
S Well I (.) the police car was outside the aerial on the back
   it was one of your vehicles which I recognised

D	CID vehicle (.) ⌈ which you ⌉ recognised
S	⌊ A white ⌋
S	A white er Vauxhall
D	Did you answer the door
S	No
D	Why not
S	I've told you I don't answer the door (.) especially at eleven twelve o'clock at night I don't answer the door

What I want to raise here is the question of what sort of activity is being performed in the policeman *D*'s arrowed turn. The policeman is saying, in slightly different terms, part of what has been said in answer to his earlier question. But in saying this what is he doing?

Activity 7.16

Consider whether the suspect considers the policeman is doing any of the following things:

- repeating what was said as an accompaniment to writing it down
- checking that he correctly heard what was said
- expressing surprise at what was said
- offering a possible version or **formulation** of what was said because what was said came across in some way as confused

Discussion

We can imagine a variety of scenarios in which a repetition of the whole or some part of the prior speaking turn could be interpretable as doing any of the activities listed. But our interest here is in determining what the suspect interpreted the policeman as doing with the words used in the arrowed turn.

In determining this we have no access to the policeman's intentions but what we do have access to is the suspect's response. And the way we respond to what is said, of course, provides evidence for how we have interpreted it. If it had been treated as an accompaniment to writing it down we might have expected no response at all from the suspect, if as a hearing check or formulation then perhaps a confirmatory *mm* or *yes*.

What the suspect in fact does is to change the way he refers to the person or persons who had called at his house on the previous evening. He switches from the expression *one of your police officers* to *people*.

Why should he do this? One reason might be that doubt is cast on the applicability of the term *police officers*. In other words the suspect treats the policeman's turn as withholding confirmation that it was indeed officers who had been the late-night callers. After all, if any one should know that it was in fact police officers who had called at the suspect's house on the previous evening then surely an investigating officer should.

Suppose that instead of producing the turn in question the policeman had asked, as he does later, whether the suspect had opened the door to his callers and in doing so had referred to the callers as policemen. He might, for example, have said:

Did you open the door to these policemen

To have done so would, of course, have carried with it the implication that it was accepted that the police had indeed been the callers. Given that he did not open the door a question about opening the door to the policemen could then be seen as requiring him to focus in his next turn on the issue of evidence for what he has just said, i.e. to indicate how he in fact knew, since he did not open the door, that the callers were in fact policemen.

And we can see that he treats the policeman's turn in this way because he reformulates what he had previously said so as to avoid the issue of necessary evidence. In his reformulation he refers to the callers as people rather than policemen. Further evidence for the fact that this is the suspect's interpretation is the fact that the policeman himself interprets the suspect's unfolding turn as an attempt to duck the issue of providing evidence for what he had previously said. We see the policeman preempting the completion of the suspect's turn with his quite explicit request for information that would constitute evidence for the fact that the caller was a policeman, i.e. the evidence of a uniform.

```
→ D   A police officer came to your door last night
  S   I had people ⌈ banging ⌉
  D              ⌊ Was this ⌋ a uniformed officer
```

So what is crucial for investigators in approaching the investigation of speech activities is first to decide just what activity has been performed. And this is in itself often a difficult matter. The main evidence for the investigator is the way in which what is said is treated by the recipients of the activity in the interaction. And this will be the starting point of most investigations of speech activities in spoken verbal interaction.

8 Patterns in speech events

8.1 Introduction

So far we have investigated the sorts of things that are going on whilst people are talking to one another. When people talk to one another we have seen that they take turns; they ask questions; they make and accept invitations; they seek clarification; they ask each other to do things; they disagree with each other; they show that they recognise each other; they tell stories to each other; they display how what they are saying can be heard as relevant; they make quips; they make changes to and repair the talk they are producing in various ways. All of these sorts of things that are going on when people talk to one another can be regarded as speech activities accomplished in and through talk.

The speech activities, as we have seen, can involve describable patterns and indeed it is precisely because there are describable patterns that participants in interaction can recognise what is going on. Now speech activities can occur as we go about other sorts of non-speech activities such as when they occur in the course of the joint activity of washing up, watching TV, eating a meal or learning to drive. In these cases the activities in question could in theory proceed without any verbal interaction. But there are episodes in all our daily lives which we clearly recognise as quite distinct and in which verbal interaction is not simply an optional extra. In these cases the episode is recognisable as an instance of verbal interaction and as nothing else.

8.2   Chats, conversations, discussions, talks

We have ways in our ordinary language of talking about these episodes of verbal interaction. We talk about people having a chat, a heart-to-heart, a meeting, a job interview, asking directions, making a telephone call, teaching a class etc. From this brief list you will see that the terms that we use to talk about episodes of verbal interaction make reference in one way or another to the kinds of situations, participants and purposes that the episodes involve. For example, teaching a class will normally occur in a particular sort of physical setting, having a heart-to-heart will normally occur when the people involved are well-known to each other and a job interview has a clear and obvious purpose. What they all have in common is that as episodes in our daily lives they begin and end with the talk that they involve. As episodes they are nothing but that talk and as such we shall refer to them as **speech events** to distinguish them from other sorts of event and from speech activities.

8.3   Participants, purposes and situations

The speech events which we are to consider are **bounded events** and characterisable according to situation, participants or purpose. The following suggests itself as a most general hypothesis about the structure and organisation of such events:

Depending on situation, participants or purpose:

  (i)   any speech event will exhibit identifiable phases;
 (ii)   within any phase of a speech event, identifiable interactional tasks will be accomplished;
(iii)   the accomplishment of interactional tasks will shape turn-taking, turn design and linguistic choices.

Let's now explore each component of this hypothesis in turn with reference to an example of a particular speech event.

Countless times each day on roadsides throughout the land motorists ask directions of passing pedestrians. Following is a transcription of such an event. The situation is a busy roadside on the outskirts of York. The motorist is male and the pedestrian is an adult female. The motorist's purpose is to find out how to get to the city centre.

Finding directions – a transcription

A   Erm (.) I seem to be (.) a bit los::t ↑ I'm↑ trying to get to Yor::k

B   Oh (.) ↑oh↑ well that's quite straight for::ward from here (.) ↑if↑ you just carry on:: <u>down</u> this road this is <u>Heslington</u> <u>Lane</u>:: ⌈ (.) ⌉just

A   ⌊ Yeah ⌋

B   carry on <u>straight</u> ahead:: ⌈ (.) the ⌉ road

A   ⌊ Yeah ⌋

B   <u>forks</u> to the left but (.) ig<u>nore</u> that just go straight ahead:: (.) and that's Broa::dway (0.5) when you <u>come</u> to the end of Broadway there are a set of traffic lights::=

A   = Ye::s ↑how↑ far's that

B   Oh:: (0.5) <u>mile</u> (.) probably

A   Go straight ahead for a mile =

B   = Yes:: =

A   Ignore:: the left ⌈ fork   ⌉

B   ⌊ Ig ⌋nore the left for::k

A   Yeah (.) then I get to some traffic lights=

B   = You ↑get↑ to some traffic lights (.) turn right at the traffic lights:: ⌈ (.)   ⌉<u>carry</u>

A   ⌊ huhuh ⌋

B   on down there that's the <u>main</u>:: road into Yor::k (.) just sort of <u>carry</u> on down there ↑you'll come↑ to some traffic lights:: ↑keep↑ in the right hand <u>lane</u>:: ⌈ (.) ⌉and

A   ⌊ Yeah ⌋

B   there are some traffic ⌈ lights::   ⌉

A   ⌊ What is ⌋ it a dual carriageway then =

B   = Yes it's a dual carriageway (.) <u>part</u> of the way anyway

A   OK

B   If you carry er ↑<u>keep</u>↑ on in the right hand lane:: ⌈ (.) ⌉you

A   ⌊ Yeah ⌋

B   come to some more <u>traffic</u> lights there's a ↑round↑ about there:: <u>you</u>'ll ↑<u>see</u>↑ (.) erm (.) <u>Clifford</u>'s <u>Tower</u> on the right::=

A   = Wha- what's:: Clifford's Tower =

B   = Yes it's a big tower on a mou::nd ↑you'll be actually::↑ <u>ri</u>ding alongsi-on the road alongsi::de (0.5) Clifford's Tower (.) ⌈ You're ⌉ in York then

A   O ⌊ k:: ⌋

B   ↑There's also↑ <u>by</u> Clifford's Tower there's a (.) car park you can <u>park</u> your car <u>there</u> and then:: =

A   OK So I look out for:: a tower on top of a mound and he

⌈ ad   ⌉ towards that:: ⌈ (.)   ⌉

B   ⌊ Ye:s:: ⌋   ⌊ Yes:: ⌋

Ye ⌈ s::   ⌉

A   ⌊ Wh ⌋ en I get in /tu::/ =

B   = ↑Yeah↑ when you get into ⌈ /ði:: ⌉

A   ⌊ Cit ⌋ y

B   ↑Into↑ the <u>city</u> (0.5) er <u>at</u> the traffic lights you'll be able to <u>see</u>:: Clifford's Tower from the traffic lights:: =

A   = OK (.) Fine (.) Thanks a lot (.) ↑Bye↑

8.4   Boundaries and phases

Activity 8.1

Identify three major phases exhibited in this speech event.

Discussion

It's obvious that this bounded event has a beginning and an end. The problem is to decide where the beginning ends and the end begins. Clearly the middle phase of this event is identifiable as the phase during which directions are given. So if we can identify where that phase begins then that will provide a basis for determining where the beginning phase ends. And it's clear that directions are begun at the following point:

(.) ↑if↑ you just carry on:: down this road this is <u>Heslington</u> <u>Lane</u>::

It would therefore seem reasonable to treat the material before this as the beginning phase of the speech event.

Identification of the beginning of the ending phase is rather more problematical. B's talk right up to A's final utterance has to do with giving directions. However, closer investigation reveals that B's talk at this point is a recapitulation of what has been said before. Moreover, it is a recapitulation done in response to A's recapitulation. So, for all practical purposes, i.e. the giving of directions, the event could have been complete at the point just before A's recapitulation. With respect to interactional purposes the event, of course, could not be properly complete at this point, so the end phase is begun with A's

> → *A*   OK so look out for:: a tower on top of a mound and head towards that:: (.)

8.5   Interactional tasks

Activity 8.2

Identify the interactional tasks accomplished during each of the three major phases of the event.

Discussion

Participants in any speech event will need to perform certain tasks so that the general and specific purposes they might have can be accomplished in an orderly, and therefore recognisable, way.

Motorists can pull in to the side of the road and start talking to passing pedestrians for many sorts of reasons. So in order to make clear what is happening, and in order to facilitate its happening, I suggest that the following necessary interactional tasks will routinely be accomplished during the opening phase of a speech event in which a motorist is seeking directions:

(i)   identification of the type of event being initiated;
(ii)   identification of a specific purpose for the event being initiated;
(iii)   identification of participant characteristics relevant to engagement in the event being initiated.

We can see all of these tasks being accomplished in the opening phase identified earlier.

Of course, our identification of what is going on here relies on our prior knowledge of who is speaking and in what situation. Thus, *I seem to be a bit lost* said by a parishioner to a priest in a confessional halfway through the confession would give rise to quite different interpretations. Here we can take it as a signal that what follows is going to have to do with seeking directions. We can also establish during this phase that the directions will be of a specific kind for immediate use. Finally, we can establish that whilst speaker A is a stranger to York, B is not. Just how we establish all this will be discussed later.

I suggest that during the second phase of this speech event the pedestrian's main interactional task will be to provide relevant directions, whilst the motorist's will be to display that they are received and understood, or that they are in need of some sort of clarification, expansion or other repair which would aid understanding. Again we can see these tasks being accomplished in the second phase we identified earlier. Speaker B gives directions, speaker A acknowledges their receipt in various ways, asks for additional information, and formulates for subsequent confirmation by speaker B what he takes speaker B to have said.

I suggest that during the third phase, which is the end phase of this event, the following interactional tasks will be accomplished:

(i)   a *concluding* display of understanding of the directions given;
(ii) a display of adequacy of the directions given;
(iii) a final disengagement from the event.

8.6   Designing turns for interactional tasks

Activity 8.3

For the first phase of the event, show how the interactional tasks of (a) event initiation, (b) event identification, (c) purpose identification and (d) participant identification shape the turn-taking, turn design and linguistic choices exhibited during the phase.

Discussion

The majority of the interactional tasks to be accomplished here are the responsibility of the motorist, and so we should expect his turns to be the more complex and extended. Passing pedestrians can have the infuriating habit of simply walking by when you crane across the passenger seat as a way of attracting their attention. As an additional way of getting someone's attention and persuading them to make themselves available for interaction in this situation, we can use some such device as *Excuse me* or, as in this case, a vocalisation like *erm*, which signals that you want to speak. The following micropause allows for the establishment of attention, but this may well not be achieved immediately. And so at the beginning of speech events we are likely to encounter hesitations and recyclings which are responsive to apparent inattention or lack of full attention on the part of the potential listener.

> *A*   Erm (.) I seem to be (.) be a bit los::t

Now, given the situation and who is speaking, the claim to be lost acts as a clear signal that the speaker is attempting to initiate a speech event, the purpose of which is to seek directions. The speaker does not seem vulnerable to loss of the speaker role until after initiation and completion of an extension to his turn. This extension is used to specify a *precise* purpose for the event and to identify himself as a stranger to the area. Notice that he does not say that he is trying to get to 'town', but rather that he is trying to get to 'York'. A person with local knowledge would be more likely to use the former rather than the latter formulation.

> → *A*   ↑I'm↑ trying to get to Yor::k

Now by this point in the interaction speaker A has initiated the event, identifies it, himself and a specific purpose. What he has not done, and what is sometimes done by first speakers, is to establish the credentials of the pedestrian with some such question as *Are you from round here?*. This, of course, is a necessary interactional task given his purpose. It may be that the motorist has grounds for not doing this explicitly – as, for example, would be the case if the pedestrian were carrying household shopping, not dressed like a tourist etc. The task in this interaction, however, is accomplished in the talk by speaker B. Her first *Oh* would seem to acknowledge her availability for interaction, i.e. it signals that she is willing to participate in *this* directions-seeking speech event. The second component of her turn indirectly establishes her credentials with respect to local knowledge, offering as assessment of the difficulty of the motorist's problem:

> → *B* Oh (.) ↑Oh↑ well that's quite straightfor::ward from here (.)

We should note that B's use of the deictic expression *from here* incorporates the assumption that the directions to be given are for immediate use and takes the current geographical position as the relevant reference point. Finally it is clear that, having characterised herself as a potential provider of the relevant directions, she assumes rights to an extended turn, during which those directions can be given.

Activity 8.4

For the second phase of the event, show how the accomplishment of the interactional tasks of giving directions, receiving directions, and clarification shape the turn-taking, turn design and linguistic choices exhibited during the phase.

Discussion

Giving directions to people in effect amounts to telling people what to do. And telling people what to do can be a delicate matter. We expect certain categories of people to be telling us what to do in the normal course of things, and we can be more or less happy with this state of affairs. Officers in the army tell subordinates, teachers tell pupils, and parents tell children what to do. In each of these cases it would be acceptable to use subjectless **imperatives** such as *Do this, Do that, Come here, Go there*. But for other situations it's not quite so straightforward. The pedestrian giving directions to a motorist has a right to be telling the motorist what to do insofar as she has been asked to do so. But the right is temporary and negotiated only for the particular interaction. So before subjectless imperatives are used to give directions, we find forms like the following which hedge on the status of the talk as telling the motorist what to do:

> → *B* (.) ↑if↑ you just carry on:: <u>down</u> this road this is <u>He</u>slington <u>Lane</u>:: (.)

The use of subjectless imperatives is thus delayed, but such forms are used subsequently once the speaker has signalled the temporary and negotiated nature of her right to use them:

→ *B*   (.) ig<u>nore</u> that just go straight ahead:: (.)

As well as telling a listener what to do when giving directions, a speaker will need to describe particular geographical features in order that the directions can be understood. We should therefore expect the directions-giver's turns to be extended by Component Activity Addition, the aim of which is to provide possibly relevant geographical information:

→ *B*   (.) ↑if↑ you just carry on:: <u>down</u> this road + (CAA) this is <u>Heslington Lane</u>:: (.)

The directions-giver will, of course, have a right to a turn which can be extended up to a point where the activity of giving directions adequate to the motorist's needs, i.e. which will enable him to find his way to York, is recognisably complete. This right can be suspended temporarily by the use of a **clarification request** by the motorist, which queries some detail of what the directions-giver has said:

→ *A*   =Ye::s ↑how↑ far's that

This turn is in fact latched on to the previous turn, an indication of A's awareness of B's continuing right to an extended turn. Up to this point A has used minimal acknowledgements at possible turn transition places as a display of understanding. Speaker A then seeks confirmation of his understanding by a series of summary formulations of the details of the directions he has been given. Confirmation of these formulations is done in the form of repeats by B of the formulations. For example:

A   Ignore:: the left ⌈ fork ⌉
→ *B*   　　　　　　　　 ⌊ Ig ⌋ nore the left for::k

When an understanding of the directions given so far has been established in this way, the directions-giver continues with another extended turn through which further directions are given and put in context. These in turn, and in similar ways, are acknowledged, queried and confirmed.

Finally, we might note that latching and overlap in turn-taking usually occur in this talk either when something is to be queried in the course of an extended turn, i.e. when there is a need to get something in, or when turn completion is highly predictable, as when a summarising formulation is being confirmed. For example:

B   (.) and there are some traffic ⎡ lights:: ⎤
A   ⎣ What is ⎦ it a dual
carriageway then
A   When I get in /tuː/ =
B   ↑Yeah↑ when you get into ⎡ /ðiː/ ⎤
                                      ⎣ City ⎦

Activity 8.5

For the third phase of the event, show how the accomplishment of the interactional tasks of (a) a final display of understanding, (b) a final display of adequacy of the directions given, and (c) final disengagement from the event shape the turn-taking, turn design and linguistic choices exhibited during the phase.

Discussion

The interactional tasks to be accomplished here are the central, though not exclusive, concern of the motorist. A's turn which begins this phase is in fact latched with B's prior and incomplete turn. It is incomplete because of the *and then::* which projects more talk. What B has said up to this point, of course, can indeed satisfy A's original purpose insofar as it has provided A with directions that would enable him to reach his destination. What A then does is to preempt further talk by producing an acknowledgement that is more than minimal. It is immediately followed, without intervening micropause, by a summarising formulation, the concluding nature of which is signalled by the initial *So*. There then follows a deal of overlapping and latching as the formulation is confirmed. A's final turn again preempts further talk by being latched, but this time the turn is extended not by further formulation, but by an assessment of the understanding achieved, a pre-terminal expression of thanks, and terminal leave-taking which finally closes the event. All of these final activities are accomplished with ritualised expressions:

→ *A* OK (.) Fine (.) Thanks a lot (.) ↑Bye↑

8.7 Telephone conversations

The second sort of bounded speech event to be investigated is the 'telephone call'. Broadly, telephone calls can be either **service encounters** or **non-service encounters**. Service encounters are, for example, calls to the doctor's surgery to make an appointment, calls to a taxi firm to order a taxi, and calls to business organisations to enquire about, order or offer products and services. Non-service encounters are, for example, calls to friends to chat, offer invitations, make arrangements etc. The call we are to consider is of the non-service kind between two women who are close friends. However, before looking in detail at this call it will be useful to consider again the call involving a deaf person considered in an earlier chapter. The call was then considered in order to illustrate certain aspects of turn-taking in conversation. We shall see that the rules which underlie turn-taking play a significant role in shaping the phases of the telephone call.

Activity 8.6 _____

Examine the transcript and identify an opening phase and a closing phase.

Niki	HELLO GA
Mother-in-Law	HI MOM HERE HOW IS NIKI TODAY GA
Niki	IM FINE MY ARM IS SORE GA
Mother-in-Law	YES THE DOCTOR SAID IT WOULD BE HOW IS YOUR TUMMY GA
Niki	I THINK IT IS FINE GA
Mother-in-Law	ARE YOU STILL IN PAIN GA
Niki	NO I DONT HAVE PAIN GA
Mother-in-Law	THAT IS GOOD TELL IAN TO BRING OVER THAT BILL YOU GOT FROM THE BANK
	AND AN OLD ONE SO I CAN SEE HOW MUCH DIFFERENCE YOU HAVE TO PAY MORE I HAVE TO KNOW HOW MUCH MORE YOU ARE GOING TO HAVE TO PAY THEM SO I KNOW WHAT IM TALKING ABOUT WHEN I CALL THEM GA

Niki	YES MY MUM JUST TOLD ME THAT U WANTED HIM TO BRING THE BILL ILL TELL HIM WE HAD XX HAVE TO PAY 16$ MORE GA
Mother-in-Law	OK I WILL CALL AND FIND OUT MORE THEY TOLD YOU IT WOULD GO UP A FEW DOLLARS RIGHT GA
Niki	YES BUT THEY GAVE US MORE GA
Mother-in-Law	I KNOW I WILL CALL AND SEE WHAT THEY CAN DO WAIT TO SEE WHAT HAPPENS ANYWAY GA
Niki	OK WHEN I DRINK TEA AND IT TASTE FUNNY IN MY TUMMY I THINK I HAVE BLEED IN MY THROAT GA
Mother-in-Law	OH WELL THE DOCTOR SAID IT WOULD FEEL FUNNY
	OK
Niki	THAT IS ALL I HAVE TO SAY GA
Mother-in-Law	OK TELL IAN TO BRING THE STUFF OVER FOR ME DAD AND I WILL BE DOWN LATER TO SEE YOU IF YOU WANT US TO BRING A X SOMETHING FOR SUPPER TELL IAN WHAT YOU WANT AND I WILL BRING IT OK GA
Niki	I THINK I WILL EAT CHICKEN NOODLE SOUP GA
Mother-in-Law	DO YOU HAVE ENOUGH GA
Niki	YES I HAVE ONE CAN GA
Mother-in-Law	OK FINE WE WILL SEE YOU LATER GA OR SK
Niki	OK WILL SEE U LATER BYE GA TO SKSKSKSKSK

Discussion

The thing that strikes me about the early stages of this call is that it follows a rather smooth and predictable pattern up to the point at which the mother-in-law says,

> *Mother-in-law* ... TELL IAN TO BRING OVER THAT
> BILL YOU GOT FROM THE BANK

It seems to me that it is at this point that the opening phase ends and the topic which is the reason for the call is being initiated. What comes before this is what you would expect in any call between friends. It doesn't seem to depend upon who is speaking to whom. What follows, however, depends crucially on who the people are and what their particular purposes are.

With regard to the closing phase of the call, it would seem to be initiated with Niki's turn,

> *Niki* THAT IS ALL I HAVE TO SAY GA

Activity 8.7

Examine the opening phase and the closing phase and identify the interactional tasks accomplished during each phase.

Discussion

When we meet someone in the street or at a party whom we recognise, we usually offer them a greeting of some sort. Among the devices we use to do this are such items as *Hello* or *Hi*. Now the word *Hello* occurs at the very beginning of this call, but we should not suppose that it is therefore accomplishing the interactional task of greeting. The *Hello* which is produced at the very beginning of a telephone call is more often than not produced by the person who is receiving the call, i.e. the called. The called is responding to the ring of the phone, which is in effect a summons to the called to make themselves available for interaction. So the *HELLO* at the beginning of the call is a response to a summons and not a greeting. In this call the called does not actually identify herself or where she is speaking from (**station identification**) within her first turn, which she uses, as we have seen, as a response to a summons.

The caller then indeed does accomplish the interactional task of greeting with her *HI*. In addition, she identifies herself with her *MOM HERE*, and incorporates a recognition of whom she is speaking to into her enquiry about the state of Niki's health, with her *HOW IS NIKI TODAY*. She assumes she knows the identity of whom she is addressing, presumably because she is responded to with the device for deaf people. Now the caller's *HOW IS NIKI TODAY* turns out to be treated by Niki as a specific enquiry into the state of her health, and hence as a possible reason for the call and as the first topic of the conversation. However, general up-dating enquiries during the opening phases of telephone calls of this sort are very common, and usually are dealt with in a routine way before passing on to the main reason for the call. Here I would suggest that a general enquiry into the state of Niki's health initiated what turns out to be a somewhat extended section of the opening phase of the call, and delays initiation of the topic which is the caller's most likely reason for the call. The enquiry then becomes a topic in its own right.

So we can see that the interactional tasks to be accomplished during the opening of a call can include greetings, station/person identification and recognition, and general up-dating enquiries.

In the closing phase of the call the participants also perform a range of activities that are in one way or another relevant to closure. Closure of the call will mean ceasing to type and switching off the apparatus by both participants. Normally turn transfer is signalled by GA. If both parties have, as it were, nothing to go ahead with, then bringing the call to a close would clearly be an appropriate thing to do. An essential task for the participants then is to signal to each other that they indeed have nothing to go ahead with. The first place in a call where signalling this is appropriate is, of course, where the current topic can be seen to be completed or approaching completion. In the call we are discussing we can see that the topic of the bank bill has been closed, and Niki then tries to reinitiate talk about her physical condition as the next topic:

> *Niki*   OK (topic closure)
> (topic reinitiation) WHEN I DRINK TEA AND IT TASTE FUNNY IN MY TUMMY I THINK I HAVE BLEED IN MY THROAT GA

The mother's turn which immediately follows does not add new information and does not require a question or clarification request format that would oblige Niki to produce further talk relevant to the topic. The mother's turn effectively proposes that all that could be said on the topic has been said, and is known, understood and appreciated by both participants:

> *Mother-in-law* OH WELL THE DOCTOR SAID IT WOULD FEEL FUNNY

There then follows a space in the typescript where nothing is typed and this amounts to a pause in the talk. What the mother had not done was to indicate turn transfer in the usual manner with GA. Turn transfer is eventually signalled after the pause with *OK*. So at this point in the call the topic which was the reason for the call has been closed, a reinitiated topic has been closed, and a next speaker, i.e. Niki, has been offered a turn of her own choice. She can do what she likes with it precisely because the mother-in-law's turn has required nothing specific of her. Niki could persist with the topic of her own physical state, which mother-in-law has proposed as closed, introduce a new topic, or signal that she has nothing to go ahead with. She takes the last of these three options:

> *Niki* THAT IS ALL I HAVE TO SAY GA

The mother-in-law then accepts this as a signal that she can proceed to close the call and she does this in three ways:

1. Explicit acknowledgement of Niki's turn:

> *Mother-in-law* OK

2. Reiteration of the reason for the call:

> *Mother-in-law* TELL IAN TO BRING THE STUFF OVER FOR ME

3. Initiation of arrangements for a next meeting:

> *Mother-in-law* DAD AND I WILL BE DOWN LATER TO SEE YOU IF YOU WANT US TO BRING A X SOMETHING FOR SUPPER TELL IAN WHAT YOU WANT AND I WILL BRING IT OK GA

These arrangements then briefly become the focus of the talk. We can say that the arrangements are thus *topicalised*. However, the very fact that the arrangements are for something that is to follow the conversation implies imminent closure of the call. As the topic of these arrangements is closed, the mother-in-law produces a turn in which she does the first part of what is a **paired exchange** – *BYE*. The other participant is to produce the second part of the pair with her own *BYE*. This we can refer to as the **terminal exchange** of the call. We should note, however, that even after the mother-in-law's *BYE* she offers Niki the option of further talk with the usual GA. In other words, the mother-in-law's *BYE* doesn't end the conversation. Things can be brought to a final close only with the collaboration and agreement of Niki. In fact, the mother-in-law at this point actually says *GA OR SK*, which means 'go ahead or sign off'. Niki takes the 'sign off' option which closes the call following her production of *BYE*.

So in the closing phase of this call we can see the participants accomplishing such interactional tasks as indicating and recognising (i) that closure is appropriate, and (ii) that a process that can lead to closure has been initiated; and collaborating to produce a terminal exchange through which the recurrent pattern of repeated turn transfer is finally suspended and the speech event closed.

Extract 5 is a recording of a telephone call, again of the non-service encounter type, and is between two women who are well-known to each other.

Activity 8.8

(i)   Identify the opening phase of the call;
(ii) explain in detail the interactional tasks accomplished during the phase; and
(iii) comment on how the interactional tasks are accomplished.

Telephone call – a transcription

(*telephone rings*)
V   Hello: seven <u>nine</u> 0 three <u>one</u>
J   Hello ↑Vera↑

V   Hallo J⌈ enny::   ⌉
J   ⌊ h·h·h·ha:: ⌋ ·h·h·h (.) ⌈ ↑I↑ was ⌉ just er ↑ring↑ing
V   up to   ⌊ Ho-   ⌋
J   say I'll be down in a moment:
V   ↑Oh::↑ goo::d (.) ↑goo::d↑
J   Yeah
V   Ye ⌈ :s: ⌉
J   ⌊ ye- ⌋
V   ↑Where↑ did you get to last night:
    (.)
J   Las-↑I↑ di- ↑I↑ didn't go ↑anywhere::↑
    (.)
V   Well ↑Matthew↑ rang to see if you were here
    (0.5)
J   ° Oh::: ° wa- ↑was↑ it ↑la:st night↑ (.) ↑yes↑ it wa- that's
    right it ↑wa:s↑ last ni. ·h·h ↑no↑ I'd taken Ivan:: erm (.) to
    /ði/ er (.) ↑sports↑ centre in ⌈ Saltburn ⌉ (.) ↑and↑ I left
V   ⌊ ·h·h Oh::: ⌋
J   a no::te (.) ↑no↑ I left a note for Matthew saying erm (.) ·h I
    I le- (.) because I know he's a little devil you know: (.) so
    ↑I↑ h·h·h· I wr- ↑left↑ a note (.) to say thay I'd be ↑back↑ (.)
    soon ·h and I put the ti:me on it ↑I↑ said I've just taken Ivan
    to the (.) centre ⌈ (.) ⌉ the sports centre ⌈ (.) ⌉ ↑erm↑ (.)
V   ⌊ mm ⌋   ⌊ Ah::: ⌋
J   Well a- what time °was it° (.) I left here about twenty to five:
V   I don't know what time it was ⌈ Jenny ⌉⌈ ↑I can't↑ remember
J   ⌊ Ye:s   ⌋⌊ I left here at twenty
       really ⌉
              ⌋ to five and there was nobody in: ↑now↑ I thought he
    would have come with me you see ⌈ ::   ⌉ now (.) then I
V   ⌊ Ye ⌋ :s
    picked Ivan up at ten /tu::/
J   (.) and then it too- ↑well↑ I had to go fairly slow to Saltburn
    with the roads being ba:d =
V   = Ye::s it would be ⌈ :: ⌉
J   ⌊ an: ⌋ d then I got back and I stopped in
    town just to buy some butter: (.) because ⌈ I   ⌉ was out of
V   ⌊ Yeah ⌋
    butter: ·h

J   and I came home: ↑we::ll↑ he was in <u>tears:</u> (.) so:: that was
    it:: ⌈ (.) ⌉ I don't know why ↑I↑ don't know what had upset
V   ⌊ mm ⌋
  him I'm
J   sure =
V   = Oh dear ⌈ me   ⌉
J   ⌊ ↑but↑ ⌋ I hadn't been gone: <u>that</u> ⌈ long ↑I↑ ⌉ was
V   ⌊ No:: ⌋
J   back ⌈ here ⌉
V   ⌊ No: ⌋
J   before six:: =
V   Oh:: <u>heck</u> (.) and <u>I</u> rang ↑Joyce↑ up last night thinking she
  was having her <u>teeth</u> out you know:: John had gone to
  <u>London</u> for an interview to see how ↑she <u>was</u>↑ (.) ↑↑she↑↑
  was out at the ↑club↑ wasn't she and left <u>Su::</u>san who's only
  ten:: ⌈ (.)   ⌉ er on
J   ⌊ ye::s ⌋
V   her own she'd be on her (xxx) <u>own</u> till about half past eleven
  (.) °last night° =
J   Oh well it's diff- ↑well↑ (.) I (.) in <u>fact</u> Kenny was playing in
  the chess tournament:: (.) and <u>he</u> didn't get in so I didn't go
  <u>typing</u> last night:
V   Didn't you: =
J   = No:: ⌈ well I sa- well I <u>ca:n't</u> ⌉ leave him for two hours if I
V   ⌊ Oh:::   ⌋
  ↑if↑
J   he's crying when I've left him for <u>one::</u>
V   Oh <u>dear</u> me
J   so I er you know:: as I say I didn't get to ⌈ typing: ⌉
V   ⌊ Aye:: you're ⌋ well
  tied down aren't you=
J   =↑Well↑ I <u>am</u> rea ⌈ <u>lly::</u> ⌉ ye:s yes ↑you know↑ because he
V   ⌊ Yeah ⌋
  does
J   ↑he <u>hates</u>↑ being in on his own ⌈ for the ⌉ pe<u>cul</u>iar rea: son
V   ⌊ Ye::s ⌋
  ↑I↑
J   mean he ↑al↑ ways knows where I'm going:: and ⌈ (.)   ⌉
V   ⌊ Yes:: ⌋
  ↑approx↑ imately

J   what time I'll be in=

V   = Ye::s

J   because I̲van said in the morning would I take him through to Saltburn and I said °well I° (.) ↑I↑ don't know the roads are still ba::d ↑I↑ ˙h˙h might h˙h˙ not ↑make it↑

V   No:: no were they v̲e̲r̲y̲ bad Jenny:: ⌈ (.)   ⌉

J   ⌊ erm ⌋ No it wasn't it's just that you can't go so fast you know ⌈ you ⌉ ↑you

V   ⌊ No:: ⌋

J   ⌈ know↑ ⌉ you just have to be:: that little bit more care:

V   ⌊ no:: ⌋

J   ⌈ ful ⌉

V   ⌊ ↑I↑ ⌋ think it's that little bit war::mer tonight =

J   Oh it is ↑it's↑ not so ba::d ⌈ (****) ⌉ q̲u̲i̲t̲e̲ as severe::

V   ⌊ It's not ⌋

J   tonight (.) no⌈ :: ⌉ but it's ↑it's::↑ (.) melted but I ↑if↑ it

V   ⌊ No ⌋ ::

J   f̲r̲e̲e̲:zes tonight it'll be wor::se tomorrow ⌈ (*****)   ⌉

V   ⌊ Tomorrow ⌋ that's the only thing:: ye:⌈ :s   ⌉ (.) ⌈ I   ⌉ think I'll stay in bed in

J   ⌊ Ye: ⌋ :s ⌊ ye::s ⌋

V   the mor⌈ ning ⌉

J   ⌊ ha ⌋ I don't ⌈ blame you ⌉ ˙h hey listen (.) ˙h you

V   ⌊ hehehehehe ⌋

J   should have come on Tuesday

V   Was it goo::d

J   Oh:: it was marvellous ⌈ ↑I↑ t̲h̲o̲r̲o̲u̲g̲h̲l̲y̲ ⌉ enjoyed it ↑yes↑

V   ⌊ Oh was it ⌋

V   Ah:::

J   mm (.) We you ↑you'd↑ have loved it::

V   Yes::

J   You know:: it was a little bit saucy h˙h˙h ⌈ and it:: ⌉

V   ⌊ haha ⌋ hahaha hahaha

J   and it was er you know was a r̲i̲g̲h̲t̲ good m̲u̲r̲d̲e̲r̲ (.) right

    ⌈ good ⌉

V   ⌊ ye::s ⌋

J   t̲h̲r̲i̲l̲l̲e̲r̲ ⌈ (.) mm::: ⌉

V   ⌊ Oh goo::d ⌋

J Ye::s (.) and it had a ↑you know↑ sort of an::: ↑it↑ <u>end</u>ed in
a great big <u>bang</u>:: ha ⌈ ha ⌉ ↑I↑ <u>jump</u>ed out of /ði/ er <u>seat</u>
V   ⌊ ha: ⌋

   I jumped
J (.) ⌈ shot ⌉ up three feet in the air I ↑think ⌈ ↑haha ⌉
V   ⌊ Oh::: ⌋   ⌊ Yes:: ⌋ (.) erm
   we didn't go to have our <u>hair</u> done by the way::
J No well I <u>gath</u>ered not ⌈ when y- (xxx) ⌉
V   ⌊ ↑a::nd↑ erm ⌋ (.) er ↑she's↑ not
   going <u>tonight</u> <u>ei</u>ther she said we'll go on <u>Monday</u> night:
J °Going where°
V (xxxxx) to have our <u>hair</u>:: done
J •h•h oh::: oh oh::: I didn't see ↑oh↑ I see:: (.) you were
   supposed to go to ↑night↑ if you w- ↑if↑ you hadn't gone ^{on}
   Thurs:: ⌈ day ⌉
V   ⌊ if ⌋ we hadn't have gone on:: <u>Wednesday</u> we ^{were}
   supposed to go tonight ↑re↑ member I said I'd <u>ring</u> you if I
   was going =
J = •h Oh I see: no I ⌈ I   ⌉ <u>knew</u> that was er <u>Wednes</u>day =
V   ⌊ but ⌋ erm
   = er she's er:: ↑she's↑ not going till <u>Mon</u>day:
J Oh:::=
V = and then Jenny I'll do it my<u>self</u> afterwards it's a bit of a
   <u>faff</u> on you know:: =
J = (x ⌈ x ⌡
V   ⌊ (x ⌡ x)
J What was the <u>mat</u>ter on <u>Wednes</u>day
V erm (.) well I think it was the ↑wea↑ther you know:: she
   didn't li- ↑feel↑ like going in the weather you ⌈ see:::   ⌉
J   ⌊ Oh:: oh ⌋
   it's- because she said she would't be going if Janno was going
   to that keep fit thing:
V That's right •h ↑well↑ I met Janno:: erm <u>yesterday</u> and she'd
   had a for::m from the Age Concern about that jo:::b
J Oh she has::
V so:: er she was sending the for::m back
J ↑Oh↑ she g- ↑oh↑ and that's good then (.) <u>pleased</u> she
   applying

V Ye::s yes she'll p- er ↑she↑ <u>rang</u> up on the <u>Mon</u>day morn-
   ing:: ⌈ you know ⌉
J   ⌊ mm::   ⌋ ↑Oh↑ good ⌈ mm ⌉
V   ⌊ and ⌋ she's got the applica-
   tion form
J Oh::: so when is the interview did you say::
V She didn't well:: she's got to send her form back =
J = Oh: ⌈ ::   ⌉
V   ⌊ she ⌋ doesn't know when the interview ⌈ is ⌉ it's just
J   ⌊ Oh ⌋
   a for::m
V No:⌈ : ⌉
J   ⌊ Ye ⌋
V No
J Ye:s •h ↑what's <u>happening</u> next doo:r↑ they moving <u>in</u> or
   moving <u>out</u> I couldn't de ⌈ ci::de ⌉ ↑ hehe ↑
V   ⌊ ↑Oh:: ⌋ no ↑er::m↑ (.) I'll tell you
   all the news when you come down ↑no↑ they're getting the
   <u>key</u>:: ↑is it the sixteenth to<u>day</u>↑
   (0.5)
J er:: ⌈ Yeah ⌉
V   ⌊ It is ⌋ isn't it=
J = er::m /ði/ erm that'⌈ s right   ⌉
V   ⌊ They're get ⌋ing the key today::
   (0.5)
   bu::-erm they'll be a little whi::le I think before they move in
   because he's a <u>handyma:n</u> ⌈ you know:: ⌉
J   ⌊ Oh::   ⌋ ↑only↑ the <u>lorry</u>
   was there this morning the <u>remo:val</u> lorry ↑and I couldn't
   decide↑ whether it was them moving out or the ⌈ the new
V   ⌊ ↑Oh::↑
   people moving in ⌉
   (.) it could be::: ⌋ erm (.) she's selling some of her fur- ↑
   she's↑ sending some of her furniture to the <u>saleroo::m</u>
   (0.5)
J Ye::s =
V =er::m (.) °<u>I</u> thought it was going on <u>We:</u>dnesday actually::°
J Oh:: =
V = so ↑I <u>don't</u> <u>know</u>↑

J   ↑Anyway <u>some</u> went today↑ <u>ob</u>viously because the <u>lorry</u> was
    there this mor::ning::

V   Yeah well that's c- ↑that↑ would be:: (.) Mrs Mar::sh's I
    should <u>think</u> =

J   = Yeah oh maybe ⌈ ↑I↑ ⌉ don't know::
V   ⌊ ye::s ⌋

J   Ye::s =

J   = but ↑I↑ just wondered if there were neighbours in or not
    yet: °h =

V   = ⌈ yes
J   ⌊ ↑Any ⌋ way↑ °h I'm just going to have a cup of tea and
    <u>then</u> I want to go <u>sho</u>::pping: ⌈ ↑so↑ (.) I'll see you later
V   ⌊ Yes ↑O:::K↑ Jenny see you

    on ⌉ then
    in ⌋ about an hour or so eh

J   Ye::s =

V   = Right

J   O:: ⌈ k
V   ⌊ Bye:: love ⌋ =

J   = ↑Cheerio↑

V   Cheerio

Discussion

The reason for the call and the first topic are introduced in the
following turn:

J   (.) ⌈ ↑I↑ was ⌉
       ⌊ Ho– ⌋

Just er ↑ring↑ing up to say I'll be coming down in a moment:

Talk up to this point deals with matters relating to the opening
of the call. In her first turn V responds to the summons accomplished through the ringing of the phone and does a station
identification:

V   Hello: <u>seven</u> <u>nine</u> 0 three <u>one</u>

We should note that V does not offer a personal identification of
herself. However, in her first turn J combines a greeting with a

proffered recognition of V implying that the sound of her voice was sufficient for the task of identification:

J   Hello: ↑Vera↑

Having done this J has in effect made the doing of certain actions particularly relevant in V's next turn. This, of course, does not mean that these actions absolutely must be done by the next speaker. It simply means that their occurrence would normally be expected and that whatever does happen next will at first be looked at to see if it can be interpreted in a way that is consistent with normal expectations. So we would expect Vera to do such things as to confirm that she is indeed Vera and perhaps to return J's greeting. In fact what she does is to return the greeting whilst in her turn proffering a recognition of Jenny and in doing this merely implies that she is indeed the person Jenny has guessed that she is:

V   Hallo J enny::

Jenny now has the task of confirming that she is indeed Jenny and in this case this seems to be accomplished through her use of laughter:

```
      V   Hallo J ⎡ enny::        ⎤
  →   J           ⎣ h°h°h°ha::    ⎦ hhh (.)
```

We should note that this confirmation is initiated as soon as there is any evidence that successful recognition has occurred on Vera's part. And this evidence we can suppose to be available at the point where the first sound of Jenny's name is recognisable in Vera's talk. This is where the laughter that accomplishes the confirmation of recognition is initiated.

   Yet another activity that is relevant during the opening phase of a telephone conversation of this type is updating with regard to each other's well-being. We see that Vera starts to do this activity immediately following the completion of recognitions and greetings. She starts this, however, in overlap with Jenny's inititation of talk in which she presents the reason for her call. The up-dating activity is therefore abandoned:

V   Hallo J⌈ <u>enny</u>::   ⌉
J   ⌊ h·h·h·ha:: ⌋ h·h·h (.) ⌈ ↑I was↑ ⌉ just er
→ V   ⌊ Ho–   ⌋
J   ↑ring↑ ing up to say I'll be down in a moment:

Activity 8.9

(i)   Identify the closing phase of the call;
(ii) explain in detail the interactional tasks accomplished during
      the phase; and
(iii) comment on how the interactional tasks are accomplished.

Discussion

A particularly interesting feature of the way in which this particular speech event proceeds is the fact that although it starts
out as something that is likely to be over very quickly it actually
turns out to be a rather lengthy affair. As was pointed out earlier
the reason for the call is given by the caller and the reason given
indicates that the call is to have just one topic, i.e. the an-
nouncement of Jenny's visit. In this way the caller types the call
as a single or **monotopical call** and so we might expect that as
soon as the participants have grounds for supposing that the
single topic has been dealt with then it is in order to proceed to
the closing phase of the conversation. But what we find here is
that the topic is indeed shown to have been dealt with to the
satisfaction of both participants but they do not then proceed to
a closing phase. Rather they proceed to talk about other matters
and in fact we see a whole series of new topics introduced and
dealt with before the conversation is finally brought to a close.

What this suggests is that if we want to identify the closing
phase of this sort of speech event then first of all we have to
identify points in the talk where a topic has been closed down.
We can see in the following fragment how the reason for call
topic is closed down:

J   ⌈ ↑I↑ was ⌉ just er ↑ring↑ing up to
V   ⌊ Ho–   ⌋
J   say I'll be down in a moment:
V   ↑Oh::↑ goo:d (.) ↑goo::d↑

→ *J* Yeah
→ *V* Ye:⌈ s: ⌉
→ *J*   ⌊ Ye- ⌋

The arrowed turns here don't add anything at all to the topic as it has been introduced. They simply provide an opportunity for the speaker of the turn to indicate that they in fact have nothing more to say on the topic and thus to indicate that the other participant can take over the speaker role. The offer of the speaker role is passed back and forth for a couple of turns before Vera takes up the option and asks a question about what Jenny was doing on the previous night. This is in effect being offered as a possible or **candidate topic** and it is then taken up or **topicalised**. So closure of the topic here does not lead to a closure of the conversation.

This pattern of topics being closed and then new topics being introduced repeats itself several times before a topic closure actually does lead to closure of the conversation. When closure of the conversation does occur it occurs as follows:

V Yeah well that's c- ↑that↑ would be:: (.) Mrs Marsh's
    I should <u>think</u> =
J = Yeah oh maybe ⌈↑I↑⌉ don't know::
V   ⌊Ye::s⌋
→ *J* Ye::s but ↑I↑ just wondered if there were neighbours
    in or not yet: •h =
V ⌈ Yes ⌉
J ⌊ ↑Any ⌋ way↑ Oh I'm just going to have a cup of tea
    and <u>then</u> I want to go sho::pping: ⌈ ↑so↑ (.) I'll
V   ⌊ Yes ↑O:::K↑
    see you later on ⌉ then
    Jenny see you in ⌋ about an hour or so eh
→ *J* Ye::s =
V =Right
→ *J* O::⌈ K ⌉
V   ⌊ Bye:: ⌋ love =
J = ↑Cheerio↑
V Cheerio

The closure of the conversation is accomplished in stages. First of all the topic of Vera's neighbours is closed down through the typical use of the minimal turn-passing items like *yes* or *yeah*. Then Jenny introduces a new topic but it is a topic of a very particular kind. The topic has to do with what she will do at the end of the call. In this way it implies that the end of the call is about to happen. We can say that the topic she introduces at this point is **closing implicative**, i.e. it implies that the closure of the call *now*, rather than at some indefinite time in the future, is a relevant issue. Vera clearly picks up on the closing implicative nature of the topic since she confirms the arrangements Jenny said were the reason for her call, does not propose any new topic, and there follows an exchange of turn-passing items before the participants proceed to say their goodbyes and so bring the conversation to a close.

Activity 8.10

A woman goes into a chemist's shop wanting something for a cough. She is served by the owner of the shop who is a male qualified dispensing chemist. Formulate and test hypotheses regarding the following as they might occur in such a service encounter speech event:

(i)   the pattern of turn-taking;
(ii) the phases of the speech event;
(iii) the interactional tasks performed during each phase;
(iv) the speech activities engaged in by the participants;
(v) the design and interpretation of speech activities.

Activity 8.11

Test your hypotheses against the evidence of the following transcription.

A visit to the chemist's – a transcription

Ch Good morning (.) can I ↑help you↑

Wo Er:: yes I w- ↑I was↑ wondering if:: erm you could give me some ad<u>vice</u> I've ↑I've ac↑tually got quite a bad <u>cough</u>
(0.5)

Ch ↑Erm↑ (.) how long have you had this <u>cough</u>

Wo 'Bout two days

Ch ↑'Bout two days↑ (.) have you had a cold before or <u>not</u>
Wo No =
Ch = No =
Wo = No =
Ch = Well what kind of a cough is it ↑is it↑ a har::d (.) dry
cough (.) or:: d- ↑are↑ you getting (.) a lot of phlegm (.) or
wha⌈ t ⌉
Wo └ N ⌋ o:: it's a sort of har::d dry cough with a sore
throat
Ch Have you got a temperature h˙h˙
Wo ↑I don't↑ think so=
Ch =You don't think so
Wo ↑No↑
Ch But you've got a sore throat
Wo Yeah (.) yeah
Ch ↑Erm↑ (.) well what I:: would <u>take</u>:: (.) would be something
like this erm (.) mentholated bronchial balsam (.) ⌈ which ⌉
└ Ye::s ⌋
Wo is a ↑<u>cough</u>↑ suppressant ⌈ (.) ⌉ which stops the cough so
└ Yes ⌋
Ch that you don't have this irritation ⌈ (.) ⌉ but at the
Wo └ Yes ⌋
Ch same ti::me (.) it's also got in what we call <u>guaithenesin</u>

⌈ (.) ⌉ which will ↑li↑quefy any mucous which might be
Wo └ Yeah ⌋
Ch (.) stuck ⌈ (.) ⌉ in /ði:/ ⌈ (.) ⌉ bronchials ⌈ ˙h˙h ⌉ so that
Wo └ Yeah ⌋ └ Yeah ⌋ └ Yeah ⌋
Ch it's doing two jobs at ⌈ once ⌉ (.) if you <u>want</u> to take it in
Wo └ Yeah ⌋
Ch hot water it's ↑also↑ <u>mentholated</u> ⌈ and ⌉ it'll release some
Wo └ Yeah ⌋
Ch (.) y'know <u>menthol</u> (.) ⌈ so ⌉ that you'll clear your
Wo └ Yeah ⌋
Ch nasal passa ⌈ ges ⌉ ˙h˙h I would have thought that that
Wo └ Yeah ⌋
Ch sounded the right thing for ⌈ you ⌉ (.) ↑How much↑
Wo └ ↑How↑ ⌋
much is that
Ch It's fifty five p
Wo ↑Oh↑ (.) well O↑K↑ erm could I take a packet of that

Ch   Thank you
      (9.0) [*sounds of till*]
Wo   Thank you

Appendix: what to do now

Verbal interaction is perhaps the most important variety of language use. It is the kind of language use that we first engage in as infants and it is the kind of language use that we have to engage in throughout our lives as human beings. Conversation Analysis has become an important branch of language study and it is the kind of analysis with which this introductory book has been concerned. It aims to study the very fine detail of what goes on when people talk to one another in order to show how our behaviour can follow describable patterns. Ultimately the aim is to demonstrate that people are in fact aware of the patterns that they appear to follow when talking to one another and that they use this awareness in making sense of one another's talk.

Having completed the activities that have been set you will now have a much greater sense of how spoken interaction is patterned. In particular you will have seen how speakers use the resources of the spoken medium in verbal interaction; how participants manage what is essentially a multi-party activity; and how people manage the resources of language to achieve their various purposes. What you should be in a position to do now is to collect your own data samples and ask similar questions to those asked of the data in this book. You will almost certainly find that you will need to constantly refine any hypotheses that you start out with. But you will inevitably come to make observations that are new and which will increase our very limited understanding of just how humans are able to make sense of each other when they participate in the highly complex business of verbal interaction. Good luck with your investigations.

Index